EVANGELIZE THRU CHRISTIAN EDUCATION

by

ELMER L. TOWNS, Th.M., D.D.

Associate Professor
Trinity Evangelical Divinity School
Deerfield, Illinois

EVANGELICAL TEACHER TRAINING ASSOCIATION
499 Gundersen Drive
Box 327
Wheaton, Illinois 60187

Courses in the Advanced (Specialized) Certificate Program

The Missionary Enterprise
Evangelize Thru Christian Education
The Triune God
Biblical Beliefs
Church Educational Agencies or Vacation Bible School
Your Bible

First Edition

Library of Congress Catalog Card Number: 78-97811
Standard Book Number: 910566-08-9
Copyright © 1970 by Evangelical Teacher Training Association

Printed in U.S.A.

CONTENTS

FOREWORD

Evangelism thru Christian education is the mandate for church growth today. Both numerical and spiritual growth result from evangelism in the church educational program. Without evangelism the educational program becomes routine and unproductive.

Few, after self-evaluation, can be proud of their evangelistic efforts. However, all church leaders and teachers should be satisfied that their evangelistic efforts have enabled those who participate in the church educational program to hear the gospel message and to face a decision concerning relationship to Christ.

Teaching content simply provides the basis of evangelism. Teaching Christian ethics merely provides guidelines for proper conduct. Neither a knowledge of the Word without acceptance of its message nor an ethical life without Christ is Christianity. Evangelism enables the Christian educator to relate content to life and open the way to eternal salvation to all with whom he works. It is evangelism which gives balance to the ministry of the Christian worker and makes his teaching and leadership effective.

The format of this book is simple to follow. Questions are raised at the beginning of each chapter. These are intended to direct the thoughtful reader to important points covered in the chapter. Footnotes are numbered and appear at the conclusion of each chapter. Also, there is a series of content review questions plus helpful questions for discussion and application. A bibliography follows the questions.

The book will be helpful reading for all Christian workers whether or not it is studied as a part of class requirements.

PAUL E. LOTH, ED.D., *President*
Evangelical Teacher Training Association

CHAPTER ONE

EVANGELIZE: MANDATE FOR TODAY

Do you know the scriptural meaning of evangelism?
Has the message of evangelism changed in the twentieth century?
What motivates you to evangelize?

Every generation moving into Christian responsibility and leadership should rethink evangelism. Though the message does not change and the gospel is always current, it is helpful to reevaluate the methods of evangelism utilized by church educational agencies to be sure the proclamation of Christ is being heard.

CONTEMPORARY METHODS

Each new generation of Christians must communicate the gospel to its peers. Methods or techniques used to do this must take into consideration contemporary society and its values. Those who would share Christ must understand those with whom they work and clearly relate to them.

New evangelistic methods often are efficient and winsome ways to witness effectively. During recent years evangelism has received new emphasis through attractive Christian literature, beach evangelism, home and professional Bible classes, camping, and campus ministry. Both time-tested methods and fresh new ways should be used to share the gospel at all age levels.

REVITALIZED ZEAL

One of the greatest dangers facing the church in evangelism is the lack of concern, and active involvement in touching the lives of others who are without Christ.

"I don't like your way of evangelism," a church member told a famous evangelist.

"How do you win souls?" the evangelist asked.

"I — I don't," was the embarrassed answer of the critic.

The wise evangelist answered, "I like my way of doing it better than your way of not doing it."

A revitalized zeal must be evidenced in church educational programs which will transform Christians into active soul winners. Those engaged in church education have a divine challenge to evangelize. They should carefully consider the guidelines and suggestions this book contains for leaders in all departments of the church who are concerned about evangelizing those they lead.

CHRISTIAN EDUCATION COMPLEMENTS EVANGELISM

Right Purpose

Christian education is more than intellectual pursuit. It aims at more than transmission of knowledge. Right teaching of the Bible leads to changing attitudes, motives, and the will. Christian teaching involves continual personality adjustment toward spiritual maturity.

Holy Spirit Dependence

Christian education, if it is to reach the life of the individual, must put its educational methods at the disposal of the Holy Spirit. It is He who regenerates individuals. The person who evangelizes will use effective methods. However, this must be done in cooperation with the Holy Spirit. Christian teachers with a passion for winning students for Christ are as dependent upon the Holy Spirit as the evangelist engaged in mass evangelism or the missionary who preaches to the native in the bush. The Holy Spirit must be present for a man, in understanding, to commit his will to God, whether in a classroom or an evangelist's tent.

EVANGELISM COMPLEMENTS CHRISTIAN EDUCATION

Just as Christian education requires evangelism, evangelism requires Christian education. Christian education must be evangelistic to keep it from becoming simply formal intellectual exercise. On the other hand, evangelism must be educational to keep it from being merely emotional and superficial.

Christian teaching often prepares an individual for the evangelist's ministry. The evangelist has a short time in which to see results. He must emphasize that "Now is the day of salvation." The teacher has the advantage of time in which to sow the Word preparatory to salvation and in which to apply the Word to varied problems. Sowing, cultivating, and reaping, steps to conversion which the Holy Spirit uses, can be the satisfying experience of every teacher who will relate teaching and evangelism.

Gaines S. Dobbins has well said, "Christianity without evangelism is spurious Christianity, and evangelism that does not seek to make full rounded disciples is counterfeit evangelism."[1]

THE MEANING OF EVANGELISM IN SCRIPTURE

Warm emotional feelings should accompany evangelism whether being carried out by the educator or the evangelist. The warm evidence of love must radiate from the soul winner. Christian teachers and leaders should manifest concern that students are born again and dedicate their lives to Jesus Christ.

One writer has defined evangelism as ". . . every possible way of teaching outside the church door to bring people to faith in Jesus Christ and membership in His Church."[2] This includes a sincere individual invitation on the part of the local church leader.

Emphasis on church membership is important. Healthy New Testament evangelism will add great numbers to today's churches. But the goal of evangelism is the conversion of the individual, not simply the addition of members to the church roll.

Though the Greek New Testament contains no word translated "evangelism," the concept and the imperative of evangelism are integral and basic to its structure. Several New Testament words clarify the meaning of evangelism.

Preach

One clarifying word is that which is often translated "preach." It is *euaggelizō* which means "to announce good tidings" or "to preach the gospel." It is clear that the word "evangelize" is really an appropriation or transliteration of this Greek word. It might be said that "to evangelize" is "to gospelize."

In Acts 21:8, Philip was designated as the evangelist, which means he went about telling the gospel. The evangelist of the New Testament was one who spread good tidings of redemption (Acts 13:32; Heb. 4:2). The teacher who proclaims the gospel and attempts to persuade men to receive Christ is an evangelist in this sense of the word.

Herald

Another word is *kērussō* which means "to herald" and is also translated "to preach or proclaim." "Jesus went about all Galilee, teaching in their synagogues, and preaching the gospel" (Matt. 4:23). The messenger of an ancient king went from village to village heralding the decrees of the king. The emphasis is on a simple setting forth of a truth; not on the response of the hearer. When one preaches in the sense of *kērussō*, he is giving out the proclamation of the gospel (Matt. 3:1; 24:14; I Tim. 3:16).

Teach

The word *didaskō* is used by the four gospel writers to describe the evangelism of Jesus. It refers to holding discourse with others in order to instruct. It means "to teach." "Jesus went about all the cities and villages, teaching in their synagogues" (Matt. 9:35). Teaching means more than announcing the truth. Teaching clarifies and illustrates. The teacher clarifies and illustrates the plan of salvation. When a person responds to the plan of salvation by accepting Christ, teaching becomes evangelism. Jesus secured eternal results through teaching and so should church teachers.

Witness

Martureō means "to bear witness." "Ye shall be witnesses unto me" (Acts 1:8). A witness in the strict sense gives evidence or substantiation of the truth. Those who witness for Jesus Christ offer their substantiation that the message of Christ is real.

The word "martyr" comes from this word. A martyr is one who gives his life as evidence that he believes the gospel. A witness is one who is dead to all other claims upon his life.

When one witnesses, he is telling others what Jesus Christ has done for him. When a witness appears on the witness stand in a legal court, the judge is not interested in his opinions or unsubstantiated testimony. A witness is to tell what he has seen, heard, or experienced. In like manner, the witness for Jesus Christ does not give his own opinion but shares what he has seen, heard, and experienced.

Disciple

The word *mathateuō* means "to disciple." Jesus has commissioned His disciples to make disciples of others. "Go ye therefore, and teach (disciple) all nations" (Matt. 28:19). The term carries the idea of converting. The term is concerned with end results. Through teaching, the converted one is made a learner or student, and therefore, a disciple.

THE DEFINITION OF EVANGELISM

Autrey has related evangelism to the evangelist's motivation: "Evangelism is to bear witness to the gospel with soul aflame, and to teach and preach with the express purpose of making disciples of those who hear."[3] John R. Mott gave a definition in the context of results: "Evangelism is the declaration of the gospel of Christ, either privately or publicly, by a messenger of God so that men might repent of their sin, turn to God, and live abundantly."[4]

Witnessing the gospel to the total personality of man in his sinful condition so that he may respond to Christ is evangelism. The following explanation is given for each phrase in this definition of evangelism.

Witnessing is sharing what has happened to us. It is what we see, feel, or experience. We share Christ who indwells us.

The gospel is the message of the death, burial, and resurrection of Jesus Christ (I Cor. 15:1-3) which a person needs to know to be converted.

The total personality involves intellect, emotion, and will. All three factors are involved in a conversion experience.

Each *man must realize his sinful condition.* This means that man can do nothing to gain merit before God, because he has broken God's law.

A man's *response to Christ* is belief and repentance. Note the order of the words. Paul describes the sequence, "How ye turned to God (belief) from idols (repentance) to serve the living and true God" (I Thess. 1:9).

OPPORTUNITY FOR EVANGELISM IN CHRISTIAN EDUCATION

Christian education is a continuing ministry. It has a continuing influence in the community. The pastor and youth leaders may change, as well as teachers, but the educational program remains. It should build the trust and confidence of the community in a church.

Christian education reaches the individual. The local church is close to the hearts of people because it is people. The church educational program is the family and church of God communicating to the entire community.

Christian education is lay centered. It is not dependent upon great preachers or poor preachers. In the educational agencies of the organized church, lay people are given the responsibility to share the Word of God. They have the opportunity to teach the Bible consistently, day by day. As teachers live among their pupils, the Word of God is personified. In classes and organizations, teacher-evangelists can relate the gospel to lives and present Christ to individuals.

REASONS FOR EVANGELISM

Evangelism is not only important and effective for teachers and leaders, it is mandatory for all Christians. The church member cannot escape responsibility. The reasons for evangelism listed below should cause the believer to examine and evaluate his own evangelistic activity.

Commanded

Jesus commanded the disciples to "go ye therefore, and teach all nations, baptizing them in the name of the Father, and of the Son, and of the Holy Ghost" (Matt. 28:19). The scope of this command included all nations. The command is also found in Mark 16:15: "Go ye into all the world, and preach the gospel to every creature." This verse makes evangelism personal. The emphasis is on winning individuals. This command to evangelism is directed to every believer. If he is not helping to win others to Christ, he is not keeping Christ's command. Paul felt this compulsion and expressed it: "I am a debtor both to the Greeks, and to the Barbarians" (Rom. 1:14). He felt the burden of God's compulsion to win others.

Sinners' Needs

The lost condition of man compels Christians to evangelize. "For all have sinned, and come short of the glory of God" (Rom. 3:23). All men outside of Christ are lost. "The wages of sin is death" (Rom. 6:23). The writer of John declares, "He that believeth not the Son shall not see life; but the wrath of God abideth on him" (Jn. 3:36). If each church member comprehended the reality of hell and the significance of God's wrath, he would dedicate himself to the winning of men to Jesus Christ.

Man's seeking for peace compels evangelism. There are many seeking spiritual peace who would never articulate this desire. Jesus has given the invitation, "Come unto me, all ye that labour and are heavy laden, and I will give you rest" (Matt. 11:28). Only the Holy Spirit knows the heart of man (I Cor. 2:11). Therefore, believers must be ever about the duty of evangelism, witnessing to men about Jesus Christ who offers rest from the burden of sin, and peace to the human heart.

Love For Christ

Love for Christ compels evangelism. Jesus was an outstanding evangelist. He preached God's seeking love and God's coming wrath. To Christians He has given the commandment that we should prove our love by obedience. "If ye love me, keep my commandments" (Jn. 14:15). Paul indicated that the indwelling presence of Jesus Christ in the believer should motivate him to tell others of salvation. "For the love of Christ constraineth us" (II Cor. 5:14). Christ is concerned about the lost, and since He indwells believers they, too, must be concerned about the lost.

Love For Others

Love for others compels evangelism. Men love their families and work hard for them. They provide for their comfort and are concerned during illness. However, this concern often is not evidenced when their spiritual condition is concerned. The greatest concern of all to a Christian is eternity. Andrew immediately after a conversation with Jesus, "findeth his own brother Simon, and saith unto him, We have found the Messias, which is, being interpreted, the Christ" (Jn. 1:41). The example of Andrew's love should motivate all believers to evangelize both loved ones and neighbors.

Example of Christ and Disciples

The example of Jesus Christ compels evangelism. Jesus continually preached to the multitudes. At other times He is in personal conversation concerning eternal matters with such people as Nicodemus, the woman at the well, the woman taken in adultery, the rich young ruler, and Zacchaeus.

After the ascent of Jesus into heaven and the coming of the Holy Spirit upon the church, the disciples were busy with evangelism. Peter, Stephen, Philip, and Paul testified in public places. There were also examples of personal evangelism such as the conversation with the Ethiopian eunuch, Cornelius, the Philippian jailer, and Lydia. The Church of Jesus Christ thrives when evangelism is foremost in the energies of Christians.

Gospel Stewardship

God has given His people a stewardship of the gospel. The message of salvation is committed to them and they are responsible to dispense the gospel according to God's directives. In the New Testament, a man who supervised an account for another was called a steward. Paul likens believers to stewards. "Let a man so account of us, as of the ministers of Christ, and stewards of the mysteries of God" (I Cor. 4:1). God loves men, but more than this, He trusts them with His good news. This responsibility can only be discharged through evangelism.

Glory of God

The glory of God compels evangelism. Jesus challenged His disciples to bear fruit (Jn. 15:1-8). Bearing fruit brings glory to God. Bearing fruit can be applied to winning men to Christ. Just as an apple tree produces apples, so a Christian produces Christians. Bearing fruit can also apply to character — the fruit of the Spirit. If Christians are bearing the fruit of the Spirit (Gal. 5:22), they will attract others to Christ. Either way, the work of evangelism is being done and this glorifies the Father.

Lack of Workers

Few are witnessing. More must evangelize. God expects all Christians to be obedient and to witness for Him. However, the sinful nature of man makes him hesitant to obey. Christ said, "The harvest truly is plenteous, but the labourers are few" (Matt. 9:37).

The primary emphasis of a church should be evangelism. Social action, education, fellowship, or community service are secondary. The growing church is the evangelistic church. Therefore, let it be busy doing that work which produces results — evangelism.

Promise of Reward

The promise of reward encourages evangelism. Paul reminds the Christians at Corinth that they must all "appear before the judgment seat of Christ" (II Cor. 5:10). Next he reminds them that knowing the "terror of the Lord, we persuade men" (II Cor. 5:11). This persuasion is evangelism. Paul, therefore, witnesses and attempts to bring men to Christ. At another place, Paul indicates, "Fire shall try every man's work of what sort it is" (I Cor. 3:13). God will evaluate a man's effort and award him accordingly. Paul says the people whom he had won to Christ in Thessalonica became his crowns, "For what is our . . . crown of rejoicing?" (I Thess. 2:19, 20). The hymn writer has taken poetic license and expressed it thus:

> Will there be any stars,
> Any stars in my crown
> When at evening the sun goeth down?
> When I stand with the blest
> In the mansions of rest,
> Will there be any stars in my crown?

SUMMARY

Christian education and evangelism complement each other. Christ was both teacher and evangelist. Those who would follow Him cannot separate the two ministries. Opportunities for evangelism in local church educational agencies are many. Added to these are opportunities for personal evangelism by teachers and educational leaders who love the Lord. The challenge to evangelize has many reasons to support it. It cannot be ignored. Evangelism is not an elective. It is a divine imperative which every believer should obey.

NOTES

1. Gaines S. Dobbins, **Evangelism According to Christ** (Nashville: Broadman Press, 1949), p. 32.
2. George Sweazey, **Evangelism in the United States** (London: Lutterworth Press, 1958), p. 19.
3. C. E. Autrey, **You Can Win Souls** (Nashville: Broadman Press, 1961), p. 7.
4. John R. Mott, ed., **Evangelism for the World Today** (New York: Harper and Brothers, 1938), Introduction.

REVIEW QUESTIONS

1. List several methods of evangelism prominently used in recent years.
2. Show how Christian education and evangelism complement each other.
3. Define evangelism.
4. How do Christian education activities provide opportunities for evangelism?
5. What are the biblical reasons for evangelism?

FOR DISCUSSION AND APPLICATION

1. Discuss the advantages and disadvantages of evangelizing through Christian education.
2. Outline a plan of evangelism for your church educational program for a full church year.
3. Should the methods of evangelism be limited to those clearly presented in Scripture such as testimony and preaching, or do you use any method which gets results?

BIBLIOGRAPHY

Autrey, C. E. **Basic Evangelism.** Grand Rapids: Zondervan Publishing House, 1959.

Packer, J. I. **Evangelism and the Sovereignty of God.** Chicago: Inter-Varsity Press, 1961.

Sanderson, Leonard. **Using the Sunday School in Evangelism.** Nashville: Convention Press, 1958.

Wood, A. Skevington. **Evangelism: Its Theology and Practice.** Grand Rapids: Zondervan Publishing House, 1966.

TEACHERS
AS EVANGELISTS

Are you equally capable as a teacher and an evangelist?
Do you regularly emphasize the need for salvation to your class?
Have you ever won one of your pupils to Christ?

Christian teaching is a high calling. It is guiding the learning experience of others. The teacher has a great responsibility when he guides pupils into the Word of God. With this responsibility comes accountability. James exhorts, "Let not many of you become teachers, my brethren, for you know that we who teach shall be judged with greater strictness" (James 3:1 R.S.V.).

But this challenge should not keep a believer from teaching. God has provided assistance. He has promised His Holy Spirit will teach through the teacher. "The Holy [Spirit] whom the Father will send in my name, he shall teach you all things" (Jn. 14:26). Later Jesus promised, "The Spirit . . . will guide you into all truth" (Jn. 16:13). Therefore, teachers have a privileged position. The Holy Spirit illuminates both teacher and pupil. The Christian teacher is a witness who also is expected to be an evangelist.

SPIRITUAL REQUIREMENTS

A Personal Experience of Salvation

God's Son died to provide salvation. The Holy Spirit works in the individual to produce salvation. The teacher who would be used of God in winning men must first experience salvation himself. He should have a knowledge that he has eternal life because Jesus Christ died for him (I Jn. 5:11-13). This personal realization will give sincerity and conviction to the teacher when he invites students to experience God's forgiveness.

Commitment to the Will of God

The work of evangelism is God's work. If God is to work through men, they must give themselves to Him. "But yield yourselves unto God, as those that are alive from the dead, and your members as instruments of righteousness unto God" (Rom. 6:13). The teacher who would evangelize must make an active dedication of his life to God. This commitment must be a daily experience of God's power. The Savior can and does give daily victory over sin. If the teacher-evangelist is to attract others to Christ, he must radiate the peace and joy of God in his life.

The teacher who would evangelize must be a good classroom teacher. If pupils do not respect him in the teaching role, they may not respond to his evangelistic role. He must be counselor, recreation guide, and friend. The teacher fills many roles, sometimes several at the same time. If he fills them well, the student will more readily respond to him as evangelist.

Neglect on the part of the teacher to exercise effectively his role as evangelist can result in tragedy even in evangelical churches. Each teacher should assess his ministry, recognizing the barriers to his effectiveness. He must then deal with them and move on to win pupils to Christ.

SPIRITUAL PREPARATION

Knowledge of the Word

God uses His Word to convict of sin (Heb. 4:12). The Word of God gives authority to the teacher. The Old Testament prophet prefaced his message with "thus saith the Lord." Teaching which is also evangelism is not expressing personal opinions, but teaching God's Word. Therefore, one of the first laws of teaching is that the teacher must know that which he would teach.

The teacher-evangelist must also know the steps an unconverted person needs to take in order to gain salvation. When a person is ready to receive salvation, one cannot spend time hunting through his Bible for verses to explain Christ's death or man's sin. A teacher must know God's plan of salvation. The verses suggested in chapter five of this text should be learned in preparation for soul winning.

A Life of Prayer

Prayer and evangelistic teaching go together. In Acts 11:5 Peter was praying from the housetop in the city of Joppa when God communicated to him the commission to go and share the gospel with Cornelius. Paul exemplified the heart of the true teacher when he said, "Brethren, my heart's desire and prayer to God . . . is, that they might be saved" (Rom. 10:1). A life of prayer should characterize the teacher-evangelist. He should use his roll book as a prayer list. The habit of talking to God about students will make it easier to talk to students about God.

Salvation comes through faith in God. The teacher also must be ready to pray with pupils who accept Christ in faith. This is a solemn moment. A person changes to heavenly citizenship. He does not need to pray audibly to become a Christian, but if he accepts Christ (Jn. 1:12) he will probably want to pray and thank God for the miracle in his life. The Christian leader should be ready to teach a person to pray.

PERSONAL REQUIREMENTS

Conviction

A teacher-evangelist must be completely convinced that Jesus Christ can meet man's deepest spiritual need. Without such a conviction, true evangelism will flounder or become only a humanitarian or educational endeavor.

The teacher-evangelist must have a conviction that every person will be lost eternally if he does not receive Jesus Christ as Savior (Rom. 5:12; 3:23). He must share the conviction that Jesus is the only Savior from sin and the only way to heaven (Jn. 14:6; Acts 4:12). The teacher who knows his present relationship with God will want each of his pupils to share this fellowship.

Compassion

Love must be the theme of a believer's life. The teacher has been redeemed by love and now should want to share the love of God with others (II Cor. 5:14). Paul had such a love for the unsaved Jews of his day that he witnessed a "great heaviness and continual sorrow in [his] heart" (Rom. 9:2). J. I. Packer expressed Paul's heartbeat this way:

> Love made Paul warm-hearted and affectionate in his evangelism. "We were gentle among you," he reminded the Thessalonians; "being affectionately desirous of you, we were willing to have imparted unto you, not the gospel of God only, but also our own souls, because ye were dear unto us" (I Thess. 2:7 ff.). Love also made Paul considerate and adaptable in his evangelism; though he peremptorily refused to change his message to please men (Gal. 1:10) he would go to any lengths in his presentation of it to avoid giving offence . . . Paul sought to save men; and because he sought to save them, he was not content merely to throw truth at them; but he went out of his way to get alongside them, and to start thinking with them from where they were and to speak to them in terms that they could understand, and above all to avoid everything that would prejudice them against the gospel . . .[1]

Such compassion drives men to urgency. There is no way to know when a man will die. Neither can we know when God shall end the opportunity for evangelism. The Bible says, "Now is the accepted time; behold, now is the day of salvation" (II Cor. 6:2). Sensitivity for unconverted class members grows in the Christian teacher as he becomes acquainted with the needs of his students. This requires sacrifice. Autrey said, "The spirit of sacrifice cannot be artificially manufactured. It must grow naturally out of contact with Jesus and a vision of human need."[2] Many Christians would rather give money for a building project or some other tangible goal than take time to go and speak to unchurched persons about Christ. The work of soul winning begins with sacrifice. We must sacrifice our time and talents to carry the message of the cross to those yet unreached. There are times when hearts are touched and a decision is imminent. A teacher must be able to recognize these times. After a class, hearts may be tender because the Word of God has been taught. If the teacher has given an invitation to remain after class to indicate a willingness for salvation, he should be prepared for this moment of decision and lead the pupil to Christ.

Concern

The teacher sincerely concerned about the salvation of his class will follow rules of courtesy and consideration of others. He will avoid offense in pressing the claims of Christ and show himself truly interested in the interests of others. Church is a good place to show friendship. Here the teacher can go out of his way to speak to a student, learn of his background, win his confidence, and establish a wholesome relationship. Packer has said of evangelism, "The right to talk intimately to another person about the Lord Jesus Christ has to be earned, and you earn it by convincing him that you are his friend, and really care about him."[3]

PERSONAL PREPARATION

Listen

The gospel is a crucial message and must be heard. But before the teacher can secure a hearing, he must learn to listen. Listening is a character-strengthening virtue to cultivate. Many things clamor to be heard and often intrude into the privacy of homes and lives. As a result, people have become experts in tuning things out. So it is important for the Christian teacher who is seeking to introduce the Lord to his unsaved students to first of all be a good listener. He can give the message better after he has secured the confidence of the student.

Act

Winning pupils to Christ involves more than being a good Christian example. Evangelism for the teacher is a definite, purposeful act of attempting to bring students to accept Jesus Christ as Savior. Teachers must make a deliberate effort to talk to each student about salvation. Since students are usually in a class for only one year, the plan of action must be implemented immediately. The teacher-evangelist must take the initiative. He must be alert to spot class members who need the Savior. He must also take the initiative to reach the unchurched with the gospel. He must seek out the lost and share his faith in Christ. A short invitation, "I'd like to see you after class," may be all that is necessary to give a class member opportunity to express a desire for salvation.

Lead

Many Christians feel as did Jeremiah when he said, "Ah, Lord God! behold, I cannot speak: for I am a child" (Jer. 1:6). Jeremiah confesses his lack of boldness to approach men. God's answer included a promise, "Be not afraid of their faces: for I am with thee to deliver thee, said the Lord" (Jer. 1:8). God is with us, so we should have boldness, for He cannot fail. Christian humility should not cause us to be fearful. We should not acquiesce to others "for God hath not given us the spirit of fear; but of power . . ." (II Tim. 1:7). The teacher-evangelist should ask God for necessary boldness to speak to his students. The early church Christians prayed for boldness, "Lord, behold their threatenings: and grant unto thy servants, that with all boldness they may speak thy word" (Acts 4:29). The teacher should remember his responsibility — the eternal destiny of his students. Whether his pupils are small children or adults, the teacher has the responsibility to lead his pupils to Christ. God answered the prayer of the early Christians. The historian Luke declares, "And with great power gave the apostles witness of the resurrection of the Lord Jesus: and great grace was upon them all" (Acts 4:33). The same power is available for the teacher today.

The fear of being offensive can become an excuse for not speaking for Christ. The gospel may offend some but it must still be proclaimed. The teacher-evangelist, however, should be careful to avoid offensive methods. He needs tact. Tact is the mental ability of doing and saying the right thing at the right time so as not to unjustly offend or anger. Jesus used tact in reaching the woman at the well (Jn. 4). He began at the natural point of attraction — the well outside of town. He asked the Samaritan woman for a drink of water. Only later did Jesus mention her sinful life. The teacher will need tact to draw students into a discussion of the Bible. A teacher must be bold, with tactfulness, in his witness for Christ.

SUMMARY

An effective teacher-evangelist must be saved and committed to the will of God in his life. He develops his spiritual life through communion with God in the Word and through prayer. His life will reveal a conviction that people are lost, a compassion to reach them, and concern enough to discipline himself to witness faithfully. Soul winning can be the experience of dedicated teachers who pursue a definite plan of evangelism.

NOTES

1. J. I. Packer, **Evangelism and the Sovereignty of God** (Chicago: Inter-Varsity Press, 1961), pp. 52, 53.
2. C. E. Autrey, **Basic Evangelism** (Grand Rapids: Zondervan Publishing House, 1959), p. 38.
3. Packer, **Evangelism and the Sovereignty of God**, p. 81.

REVIEW QUESTIONS

1. What spiritual requirements and preparation are needed by a teacher-evangelist?
2. State the importance of prayer in evangelism.
3. What personal requirements and preparation are needed by a teacher-evangelist?
4. What are the evidences of a passion for souls?
5. How is tactfulness in evangelism shown by a teacher?

FOR DISCUSSION AND APPLICATION

1. Endeavor to list the characteristics of the person who was instrumental in bringing you to Christ. Compare these characteristics with those of others known to be effective soul winners to see if any characteristics are common to all.
2. Evaluate your personal spiritual life to determine to what degree you have the conviction, compassion, and concern necessary to be a teacher-evangelist.
3. Try to list all the contributions of church teachers toward your decision for Christ. Include times of teaching regarding salvation, personal witness, invitations, and similar ministries.

BIBLIOGRAPHY

Dawson, David M. **More Power in Soul Winning.** Grand Rapids: Zondervan Publishing House, 1952. Chapter 1.

Olford, Stephen. **The Secret of Soul-Winning.** Chicago: Moody Press, 1963.

Rice, John R. **Why Our Churches Do Not Win Souls.** Murfreesboro, Tenn.: Sword of the Lord Publishers, 1966.

Sizemore, John T. **The Ministry of Visitation.** Nashville: Convention Press, 1954. Chapter 4.

Trumbull, Charles G. **Taking Men Alive.** Westwood, N.J.: Fleming H. Revell Co., 1960.

Whitesell, Faris D. **Great Personal Workers.** Chicago: Moody Press, 1956.

CHAPTER THREE

FOUNDATIONS
OF EVANGELISM

Why should you use Scripture in leading a person to Christ?
Could you evangelize if there were no Holy Spirit?
If you do not tell about Jesus, how will God make the message known?

The Bible gives principles of evangelism. Both the *message* and the *method* are found in Scripture. Bible principles are applicable to every age in every culture, and should direct the method of evangelism.

THE WORD OF GOD — INSTRUMENT OF EVANGELISM

The Bible is the record of God's revelation of Himself to His people. It presents the goals of evangelism and is the dynamic for it. True evangelism must be based upon the Word of God.

Jesus used the Scriptures in conversation with individuals as well as in His teaching. In the synagogue in Nazareth Jesus was found reading the Word of God. After reading Isaiah 6:1, 2, he began to explain to His hearers how the Scriptures were being fulfilled (Luke 4:16-21). Jesus' basic approach to preaching and teaching was an explanation of the Scriptures. After the resurrection, Jesus walked with two of His disciples to Emmaus, "And beginning at Moses and all the prophets, he expounded unto them in all the scriptures the things concerning himself" (Luke 24:27). He used illustrations, parables, object lessons, current events, and questions. All was directed to help the pupil understand the Word of God. Evangelism through teaching has not changed in the twentieth century. Bibles should be needed in every Sunday school lesson. The well-prepared teacher leads his students into the Word of God.

The teacher who would evangelize must explain the Bible in his witness to individual pupils concerning Christ. He must provide a clear mental understanding. The Holy Spirit provides the spiritual understanding, but He does it through the Word of God. Successful evangelism through Christian education results from the Spirit of God using the Word of God through the teacher of God to reach the heart of the unconverted pupil. The Bible is the instrument used by the teacher and God in bringing healing to the unconverted, just as medicine may be the instrument used by a doctor to bring health back to the sick.

To Convict

Conviction of sin comes through the Scriptures. "For the word of God is quick, and powerful . . . and is a discerner of the thoughts and intents of the heart" (Heb. 4:12). The Word of God lays bare the sin that is hidden in the thoughts of man. God already knows the sin is there, but the Word of God convicts by illuminating the mind concerning the sin and shows an individual his sinfulness. But some people have hard hearts. "Is not my word like as a fire? saith the Lord; and like a hammer that breaketh the rock in pieces?" (Jer. 23:29). God brings conviction even to the hardest heart and causes the person to comprehend how far short of God's standard he falls.

Packer stresses that, "To be convicted of sin means to realize that one has offended God and flouted his authority, and defied him and gone against him . . ."[1] Because of rebellion, man stands condemned under God. Conviction is evidenced when the concerned person becomes aware of his wrong relationship with God, and sees his need to be restored to a relationship with God. Packer says further, "Conviction of sin always includes conviction of sins: a sense of guilt for particular wrongs done in the sight of God."[2] We see ourself as apart from God and, recognizing the result of specific sinful actions, are sorry. "Conviction always includes conviction of sinfulness: a sense of one's complete corruption and perversity in God's sight."[3] Conviction completely disorients a person. No teacher can cause conviction unaided. There is a need for a completely new heart because of the utter corruption and perversity of the sinner in God's sight. Conviction comes through the Word of God, therefore, teaching-evangelism must communicate the Scripture.

To Convert

The Scripture is said to convert a soul (Ps. 19:7). This conversion results in a changed life in the man. The source of this changed life is the Word of God. The converted man makes an about face and turns to God.

The teacher engaged in evangelism should be sure that the Word of God is understood and communicated. It is not illustration, rational process, nor forceful logic that wins souls. Even salesmanship is not enough. Only the Word of God can do the work of God in conviction and conversion.

For Eternal Life

God uses the Bible to give life. When a man is born the first time, he is given earthly life. Jesus said to Nicodemus, "Ye must be born again" (Jn. 3:7). When a man is born the second time, he is given eternal life. God uses the Bible as an instrument through which to give eternal life to man. Peter recognized the Bible as the source of eternal life. "Being born again . . . by the word of God, which liveth and abideth forever" (I Pet. 1:23). Therefore, it is through God's Word that we receive eternal life.

Jesus is God (Jn. 1:1). When He was upon the earth, He spoke many things. Jesus indicated His words were instruments through which the Holy Spirit could give life, "It is the spirit that quickeneth; the flesh profiteth nothing: the words that I speak unto you, they are spirit, and they are life" (Jn. 6:63). The Word of God gives life, whether spoken by Jesus upon this earth or written on the pages of Scripture.

To Cleanse

"Now ye are clean through the word which I have spoken unto you" (Jn. 15:3). The Lord here expressly states that cleansing from sin comes from His Word. Jesus speaks of "abiding in me" (vs. 4) as the appropriation of cleansing. People are not forgiven just because they hear the Word of God. There must be the appropriation of it. The teacher-evangelist, therefore, must communicate clearly the Word in order that it can be understood and applied.

For Faith

"So then faith cometh by hearing, and hearing by the word of God" (Rom. 10:17). The Bible is a sure foundation upon which one may root his faith. Without the Word there can be no ground for faith. But one cannot make the Word the foundation of his faith unless he hears and understands the Scripture. This message must be received and believed in order for it to be operative in the life of an individual. The stability of any pupil's faith comes from Christian teaching, based upon the written Word.

To Sanctify

Sanctification means "to set apart to God," "to make holy." The Word of God is a means through which the pupil may be sanctified. Our Lord in His high priestly prayer asked, "Sanctify them through thy truth: thy word is truth" (Jn. 17:17). Christ also gave himself for the church "that he might sanctify and cleanse it with the washing of water by the word" (Eph. 5:26). So it is, that along with cleansing His Church from the guilt and power of sin through regeneration or the washing of water, the Word is also an instrument through which the believer is cleansed from inherited sin or made holy.

This is the dynamic of God's Word. The teacher must know the Word, must experience its power in his own life, and must be convinced that "it is the power of God unto salvation to every one that believeth . . ." (Rom. 1:16). The teacher must accept it as infallible and authoritative (II Tim. 4:16). The teacher gives out God's Word and through it God speaks to the students and enlightens their hearts. There is no other book upon which the teacher can rely to change the lives of his pupils. The Word is relevant to the needs and situations of each pupil today. Frank Gaebelein said the data for Christian education is found in the Scripture and it is our duty to derive from it a "Christian view of teaching and learning," because "ours is the religion of the Book . . ."[4] The basis of true evangelism is the message of the Word of God.

THE HOLY SPIRIT — AGENT OF EVANGELISM

The unsaved person is unable to discern the meaning of the gospel. The Scriptures teach that Satan has blinded the unsaved man, rendering him incapable of perceiving the good news. "But if our gospel be hid, it is hid to them that are lost: In whom the god of this world hath blinded the minds of them which believe not" (II Cor. 4:3, 4). (Eph. 1:18; 3:5). Because of this most people do not realize their lost condition. Even when they are warned of the judgment of God to come, they have little concern. An indifferent and neglectful attitude toward eternity is common today. But these unconcerned people must be reached for Christ.

Teaching which is effective for evangelism must have a dynamic far greater than necessary for simple communication of facts. The mechanics of teaching are impersonal laws to be followed in the classroom. The dynamic for teaching is the Holy Spirit. Apart from His ministry, the teacher's best intention, motives, and methods will fail. With Him teaching can be evangelistic for He is the agent of evangelism.

For Conviction

Before man can be converted, the gospel must be understood. The Holy Spirit convicts the world of sin (Jn. 16:8). Conviction is more than mental agony or sorrow for sins, although these may follow. Conviction illuminates the mind concerning facts. The Holy Spirit causes the sinner to see that he is actually guilty before God, having broken His laws and having come short of His perfect standard (Rom. 3:23). Conviction causes the sinner to realize he has not believed in Christ (Jn. 16:9).

The unsaved man will remain in his lost, sinful condition if he rejects the Son of God (Jn. 3:18). All men are sinners, but Christ died for all. The main issue for the sinner is what he will do with Jesus. When the Holy Spirit convicts of unrighteousness (Jn. 16:8), he causes men to see Jesus Christ as the only righteous one (Jn. 16:10). Only the work of the Holy Spirit can cause the unconverted to understand that the righteous Christ died for unrighteous man. A man unaided by spiritual help cannot understand his condition before God, because he does not comprehend spiritual truth (I Cor. 2:14).

Finally, the Holy Spirit convicts of judgment (Jn. 16:8). This passage refers to God's judgment on sin at the death of Christ (Jn. 12:31, 32; II Cor. 5:21). When the Holy Spirit convicts concerning judgment, the sinner understands that Christ's death was a judgment upon the sinner's sin.

For Conversion

Regeneration is the work of the Spirit whereby life is imparted in response to faith. The Scriptures point out man is spiritually dead and separated from God by sin. "And you hath he quickened, who were dead in trespasses and sins" (Eph. 2:1). By the miracle of regeneration, the soul is given eternal life. Our Lord describes this granting of eternal life as being "born again" (Jn. 3:3). The Holy Spirit is the One who gives life to the soul when a person believes and places his faith in Jesus Christ. No amount of good resolutions can make a regenerate person. The Holy Spirit must work in the heart as the Word of God is heard and believed. As the new birth takes place, eternal life is imparted. "He that believeth on the Son hath everlasting life" (Jn. 3:36). "Not by works of righteousness which we have done, but according to his mercy he saved us, by the washing of regeneration, and renewing of the Holy Ghost" (Titus 3:5).

For Guiding Into Truth

When the Word is faithfully given out, the Holy Spirit uses the Word and applies God's message to the need of the pupil. The Holy Spirit impresses upon the pupil that there is no other truth but Jesus Christ. As the Word is faithfully taught, the unsaved pupil is brought in contact with certain truths. Pupils are enlightened through the working of the Holy Spirit, regarding their sin, Christ's righteousness, and the judgment of sin. "The Spirit places the truth in a clear light before sinners so that it may be seen and acknowledged as truth."[5]

The Holy Spirit is the agent, carrying out salvation in every heart. Halford Luccock has said, "The Holy Spirit is the present tense of God . . ."[6] God is presently working in the heart and life of every individual through the person of the Holy Spirit. The actual transformation of any pupil will come as God's Spirit moves in the class.

MEN — THE MESSENGERS OF EVANGELISM

God uses human messengers to carry the Word of God to the lost. "How then shall they call on him in whom they have not believed? and how shall they believe in him of whom they have not heard? and how shall they hear without a preacher?" (Rom. 10: 14). In these verses God speaks of the human responsibility of carrying the divine message. God's plan is to work through persons.

Their Call
Evangelists

God gives men to the church for evangelism. "And he gave some, apostles; and some, prophets; and some, evangelists; and some, pastors and teachers" (Eph. 4:11). God sets aside servants in every generation. God selects these special servants and endows them with a special gift (capacity or ability) of ministry to the church. One of these abilities is the gift of evangelism. Great evangelists fulfill a clear need. These men are gifts of God to the whole church.

Laymen

Evangelism is not restricted to the evangelist. All Christians should be doing the work of an evangelist. Not all are called to distinctive services, but God's imperative for each Christian is to win others to Christ, "Ye shall be witnesses" (Acts 1:8). Paul exhorts Timothy, "Do the work of an evangelist" (II Tim. 4:5). The evangelists are to encourage and work with laymen. None can give an excuse for not being busy with evangelism.

In the early church "they that were scattered abroad went everywhere preaching the word" (Acts 8:4). Notice the historical situation in Acts 8. Those who went about preaching or telling were not the apostles. They were laymen who were scattered from Jerusalem. They proclaimed their faith by word of mouth, on a person-to-person basis. Witnessing is one of the inalienable rights of every Christian. We should not desire a special gift, for we have a special command in the Bible. God commissions us to witness. With God's commands are his enabling gifts. If God has given the responsibility of a position in Christian education, He will also give the ability to carry out the task of evangelism.

Their Importance

Words used in the Scripture in reference to believers indicate how important is the place of men in evangelism. The following list is indicative of the relationship of believing and telling others.

Fishers of men — "I will make you fishers of men" (Matt. 4:19).

Witnesses — "Ye shall be witnesses unto me" (Acts 1:8).

Ambassadors — "We are ambassadors for Christ" (II Cor. 5:20).

Stewards — "Stewards of the mysteries of God" (I Cor. 4:1).

As an ambassador for Christ, the layman should seek out the lost and witness to them about Christ. Every leader is a steward of biblical truths — prominent among which is God's way of salvation.

SUMMARY

The Bible is the foundation for evangelism in teaching. The Holy Spirit's power proceeds through the Word of God. Therefore, evangelism must be carefully based on Scripture. Such evangelism is a ministry with which the Spirit of Truth can cooperate for eternal results.

The Holy Spirit dynamically works in the hearts of men to bring them to a saving knowledge of the Lord Jesus Christ. The Bible is the instrument through which God the Holy Spirit operates with convicting power in the hearts of lost men and women.

In God's divine program of redemption, man stands as the important figure. Man is to be saved from sin and thus the object of grace. Also it is man whom God calls to be the messenger of evangelism and share the gospel message with those who are without Christ. God uses men more than methods in proclaiming the message of redemption.

NOTES

1. J. I. Packer, **Evangelism and the Sovereignty of God** (Chicago: Inter-Varsity Press, 1961), p. 61.
2. **Ibid.**, p. 63.
3. **Ibid.**
4. Frank E. Gaebelein, "Toward a Philosophy of Christian Education," **An Introduction to Evangelical Christian Education**, ed. by J. E. Hakes (Chicago: Moody Press, 1964), p. 37.

5. Roy B. Zuck, **The Holy Spirit in Your Teaching** (Wheaton, Ill.: Scripture Press Publications, 1963), p. 39.
6. As quoted by Jesse M. Bader, **Evangelism in Changing America** (St. Louis: Bethany Press, 1957), p. 51.

REVIEW QUESTIONS

1. In what ways does the Bible serve as the instrument of evangelism?
2. In what ways does the Holy Spirit serve as the agent of evangelism?
3. Compare the ministry of evangelists and laymen in witnessing.
4. List several terms by which believers are called which show the responsibility of men to share the gospel.
5. What is the relationship of man and methods in evangelism?

FOR DISCUSSION AND APPLICATION

1. The evangelist is called a fisher of men, a witness, an ambassador, and a steward. Name several other occupations which might picture the work of an evangelist.
2. Cooperatively prepare a statement summarizing this chater. The statement might begin: "Successful evangelism through Christian education results from _____."
3. In the educational program of your church show how the Scripture, the Holy Spirit, and you are or can be related in bringing people to salvation.

BIBLIOGRAPHY

Chafer, Lewis Sperry. **True Evangelism.** Wheaton, Ill.: Van Kampen Press, 1919.
Little, Paul. **How to Give Away Your Faith.** Chicago: Moody Press, 1966.
Potts, Edwin J. **Evangelism in the Sunday School.** Wheaton, Ill.: National Sunday School Assn., 1960.
Wood, A. Skevington. **Evangelism: Its Theology and Practice.** Grand Rapids: Zondervan Publishing House, 1966.

TEACHING
FOR CONVERSION

CHAPTER FOUR

Is your classroom arranged to help you evangelize?
How does your teaching relate to evangelism?
Would those you teach consider you interested in evangelism?

Christian education is concerned with building attitudes, understandings, and character that will glorify the Lord. However, an individual cannot be taught to live a Christian life until he is in a right relationship with the Lord. If this relationship is to exist, he first must be convinced that he is a sinner and needs a Savior. The demands of God's Word for salvation must be clear if conversion is to follow.

RELATIONSHIP OF CHRISTIAN EDUCATION AND EVANGELISM

Evangelist C. E. Autrey has well said, "Men are not saved by the teaching process but the teaching process prepares man for a saving experience with God."[1] The Christian teacher must teach for conversion.

Provides Contacts

The educational agencies of the church are the most logical places for evangelistic ministry in the twentieth century. New communities seem to appear everywhere. An alert church will recognize these communities as opportunities for Christian education outreach to entire families. When families move, former ties are cut. These people often are open to a church in their new neighborhood which has a program for the total family and reflects an active interest in them. Christian education programs such as youth meetings, club ministry, camping, instruction for young parents, and leadership training attract people to a church and place them where they can hear the gospel. Once related to the church through the educational program, these families find Christian education the principal evangelistic force. The continuing opportunities it provides for witness often make the church educational program also the church evangelistic program.

Prepares for Conversion

Children in our Christian education agencies must receive a systematic study of both the Word of God and the great truths of our Christian faith. Whether or not conversion occurs immediately the leader can pave the way for the Holy Spirit to make clear the message of salvation. In the Christian education program, every student can participate in a time of worship, study, or activity with God's Word. In a good educational program, the Bible is more than heard by a passive listener; it is explored by an interested person. Christian education has unlimited ways of presenting the claims of Christ to a student. When there is involvement by the pupil with the Word of God, lives are changed. Teaching that produces conversion is effective teaching. This is Christian education at its best.

THE TEACHER AS EVANGELIST

A capable teacher can produce an evangelistic atmosphere in the classroom. He should be concerned for the salvation of his pupils, and confront them with the claims of Christ in the course of his teaching. The Holy Spirit often uses this knowledge of Christ's claims as a basis on which to move in the lives of the students.

Prayer

The teacher must prepare the environment of the class by personal prayer. He should ask for God's presence and anticipate it in the class. This feeling of readiness and expectancy comes when both teacher and pupil have asked God to work. The teacher may find great help in keeping a prayer list of each pupil. He should pray for them individually, systematically, and regularly.

Personal Concern

A teacher must be alert to class needs and be sensitive to these in presenting the lesson. One pupil may come in search of salvation, another in need of assurance in the Christian walk, and still another may be seeking friendship. Pupil needs are real and therefore must be met realistically through the study of God's Word and the application of it to these needs.

Apply Message

There is no teaching without learning. Unless change takes place in the life, the pupil has not learned. He may repeat Bible verses or even verbalize a prayer for salvation, but if there is no inner change, there is no spiritual learning. This can be change in feeling, understanding, appreciation, or emotions.

Experience is necessary for learning and evangelism. Experience is personal. No one can be a substitute for another. An experience that produces learning or leads to evangelism must involve perception by the pupil. He must understand the meaning of the gospel before he can respond. This learning experience is a step toward salvation. If true learning takes place, the lesson not only becomes a part of the pupil's life, but continues to affect it. The pupil may forget some of the facts in the lesson, but they already have added to the impact on his life.

TEACHING FOR CONVERSION

Teaching is more than telling facts or communicating knowledge. It includes guiding learning activities. The teacher-evangelist should be guiding the pupil into learning experiences that prepare him for salvation, lead him to Christ, and establish him in his faith.

Importance of Surroundings

Conversion may take place in many places other than the classroom. However, the classroom can be prepared to contribute to evangelism. Color and beauty provide a feeling of warmth, welcome, and order. Often classrooms reflect the attitude of the church toward its students. One classroom may say, "Study of the Bible is important," while a cluttered, neglected classroom encourages disrespect, and disinterest in the Bible. The atmosphere of the classroom can't produce conversion of a pupil, but it can contribute to the attitude he has toward the Word of God. This attitude is important in conversion. Lighting, heating, ventilation, and temperature need attention in order to provide comfort during the study time. A classroom which is attractive, neat, and orderly will encourage study and activity from the students and encourage orderly consideration of the claims of Christ.

Variety in room arrangement adds spark to the room and often to lesson interest. Pupils feel a freedom to discuss and contribute opinions when they are arranged in ways conducive to discussion. Appropriate arrangement of seating will permit students to speak to one another and allow the teacher to become a member of the group. The teacher becomes a guide to the student in search of truth. Greater interaction from this type of arrangement can have a lasting impact on a life. The student who voluntarily inquires regarding salvation during a discussion clearly evidences an interest which should not be neglected.

The evangelistic teacher joins with pupils around the Bible, the real authority in Christian teaching, to explore its contents.

When God provides opportunity, the teacher should use the occasion to lead a pupil to Jesus Christ.

Children's classrooms should provide centers of interest. Equipment must be usable by children and built for their size. Materials must be attractive and usable. Rooms painted with pleasing pastels have an attractiveness which may enhance the attractiveness of the message.

Just as the sanctuary says, "Worship," the classroom for youth and adults should say, "Study." If the room has an ample supply of books and audiovisual materials, this concept will be helped. This kind of classroom invites people to think, to study, and to dig deep into God's Word. It produces exciting search which may lead to conversion.

Importance of Right Procedure

Some teachers make the gospel too complicated. Pupils do not listen to lessons because the teacher is not communicating. But the gospel is simple. If the teacher is to win souls, he must add nothing to it. Its simplicity, however, does not take away from the need to study and challenge class thinking. The teacher's first responsibility is to teach the gospel. He must reduce it to its simplest essentials until it is grasped by his listeners.

If his teaching is to have lasting results, the teacher must plan his study and class presentation. This lesson plan varies for different groups and ages since teaching must adapt to varying situations and individuals. A teacher who would evangelize must have a motivation similar to that of the Apostle Paul who became all things to all men that he might by all means save some (I Cor. 9: 22). Slipshod preparation produces an impression that the gospel is unimportant. Few are won to the Lord this way.

Preparation

The following plan for preparation and study is based upon Findley B. Edge's suggestions in his book, *Teaching For Results*.

Select a definite time for study. Ask yourself these three questions: (1) What introduction should I use to capture the attention of the class? (2) What illustrations should I use to drive home the point? (3) How can I make this lesson personal to each student?

Find a definite place for study. This place must be conducive to prayer, meditation, and study. It is best to keep the materials in the room. It is frustrating and exasperating to rummage through the house looking for curriculum material.

Get some study helps. The teacher should have at least two good Bibles — one in a modern translation. Secure at least one good commentary, a Bible dictionary, and a concordance. Build a file or folder on each student in the class. Include in the file information on the individuals' interest, needs, abilities, and background, as well as experiences.[2]

The teacher must also have an inner preparation if he is to be effective. A teacher must be physically fit if he is to be excited about the lesson. The teacher also must be mentally alert and spiritually prepared. This triad (mental, physical, and spiritual) must be working together, because each affects the other and all affect teaching. The lesson must first get through to the teacher. Only then will it get through to his pupils.

Presentation

Paul had a strategy in teaching. "He engaged the audience or the individuals' attention, captured interest, set out facts, explained their significance . . . and showed how the message has been effective in a life."[3] Forethought must be given to organizing classroom strategy.

Consideration must be focused on individual needs. A helpful question or illustration by the teacher might be the bridge to reach the pupil's perplexity. If the teacher tries to solve a problem he recognizes his pupils face, the approach might clear the very obstacle which is hindering a pupil from gaining salvation. Careful lesson presentation by a teacher who knows his pupils well is an aid to evangelism.

Additional help in the preparation and presentation of a lesson plan is available in E.T.T.A. textbooks, *Understanding Teaching* and *Teaching Techniques.*

TEACHING FOR DECISION

At one time the church educational program, especially the Sunday school, was centered in evangelistic emphasis. Dwight L. Moody was a teacher-evangelist before he became a preacher for he won the boys of his Sunday school class to Jesus Christ. Many who now teach in the church educational program accepted Christ in Sunday school or vacation Bible school. This same evangelistic emphasis should be prominent in present educational programs. Too frequently evangelism is omitted as an educational goal. Facts are absorbed and recited but lives remain unchanged. Church educational programs should emphasize both teaching and evangelism — both conversion and growth.

Urgency Needed

With teaching must be the sense of urgency to bring to pass decision, ever aware that "We are the spiritual attendants, the human assistants of God in this great drama of rebirth."[4] Only thus are teachers "able ministers of the new testament" (II Cor. 3:6). The teacher has a grave responsibility to present the way of salvation to his pupils and to give each one an opportunity to accept the Lord. Some teachers may do this by emphasizing to students their need to consider God's offer. Others may simply regularly suggest the importance of a personal decision and offer assistance to anyone who is ready. It is the Spirit of God alone who finally persuades.

Continual Witness

The teacher has the opportunity continually to seek the lost in his class. He knows the difficulties each faces and the obstacles to conversion and can consistently apply the lesson according to these needs. He is alert to the awakening of a pupil in spiritual concern and is ready to invite the student to make a commitment to the Lord Jesus Christ.

Inviting to Salvation

An invitation to accept Christ, however, may be a door to salvation or an obstacle to decision. The following ways of inviting class members to come to the Savior have been used successfully by some:

A simple invitation to remain after the lesson period to discuss salvation with the teacher will provide an opportunity for the seeking individual to accept the Savior.

The alert teacher may observe a child's concern during the lesson time and purposely visit in his home during the week.

A card given to each pupil on which he can write any question with the suggestion that he may inquire regarding salvation will assist some to investigate how to come to Christ. Any inquiries should be followed up before the next class.

An informal question from the teacher as a child leaves the classroom will reveal a pupil's interest and often open the way for fuller consideration.

A careful explanation of salvation during a lesson with prayerful meditation by class members may lead to decision. The teacher then would tell any who had decided to receive Christ to make this decision known to him.

Pressure should not be imposed upon the pupils but deep interest evidenced on the part of the teacher. Carefully presenting the Word, encouraging decision, and nurturing each student often will be all the teacher can do until the Spirit of God prepares a heart for decision. At that time the teacher must be alert to the readiness and give opportunity to receive the Savior.

In inviting others to decide for Christ, the teacher must remember some helpful principles.

Make the invitation clear. Explain to the pupil what he should do and why.

Evidence confidence. The teacher who has had an experience of salvation knows that Christ can give life and should show it.

Be considerate. Never embarrass the pupil or cause anger or resentment. This will encourage continual resisting of the claims of Christ.

Be earnest. Invitations must be given earnestly. The teacher should plead as a dying man with dying men.

Group invitations should not be a substitute for personally dealing with pupils. A personal invitation may have a warmth that bowed heads and raised hands cannot produce. The time and method of invitation should be the result of the Lord's leading.

SUMMARY

The agencies of Christian education should be closely linked to an evangelistic thrust. They provide the contact with people and prepare the person for conversion. The Sunday school is the key agency, hence the teacher is an evangelist. The teacher prepares the student for conversion by providing the appropriate atmosphere and preparing himself for teaching. It is the teacher's responsibility to set forth the Word of God, and offer salvation through the Lord Jesus Christ to the student. In the light of the value God set upon the soul, evangelism must be given an important place in the church educational program.

NOTES

1. C. E. Autrey, **Basic Evangelism** (Grand Rapids: Zondervan, 1951), p. 92.
2. Findley B. Edge, **Teaching For Results** (Nashville: Broadman Press, 1956), pp. 157-160.
3. J. I. Packer, **Evangelism and the Sovereignty of God** (Chicago: Inter-Varsity Press), p. 48.
4. Samuel Southard, **Pastoral Evangelism** (Nashville: Broadman Press, 1962), p. 3.

REVIEW QUESTIONS

1. What determines whether or not the evangelistic thrust in Christian education is effective?
2. What attitudes must a teacher have to equip him to be an evangelist?

3. How do different classroom settings aid or hinder evangelism?
4. In what ways does lesson preparation contribute to evangelism?
5. What are four helpful principles to remember in giving an invitation?

FOR DISCUSSION AND APPLICATION

1. Visit a Sunday school and observe the evangelistic efforts. These would include references to salvation in a lesson and any invitation or suggestion of decision. Indicate how you would have emphasized evangelism.
2. Prepare from observation a list of ways evangelism is being emphasized in the educational program of the church you attend. Make a list of additional ways which could easily and readily be used.
3. On a lesson outline for any lesson you have taught or plan to teach, underline in a different colored ink each evangelistic point and/or opportunity for decision by class members.

BIBLIOGRAPHY

Bowman, Locke E., Jr. Straight Talk About Teaching in Today's Church. Philadelphia: The Westminster Press, 1967.

Edge, Findley B. Teaching for Results. Nashville: Broadman Press, 1956.

Gangel, Kenneth O. Understanding Teaching. Wheaton, Ill.: Evangelical Teacher Training Assn., 1968.

Joy, Donald M. Meaningful Learning in the Church. Winona Lake, Ind.: Light and Life Press, 1969.

Leavitt, Guy P. Teach With Success. Cincinnati: Standard Publishing Co., 1956.

LEADING
TO A DECISION

How would you answer a person who asked why you are a Christian?
Could you explain the way of salvation in three minutes?
If a person asked you to pray for his salvation because he couldn't pray,
what would you do?

Christ is the heart of the evangelistic message. One of the greatest joys of the Christian life is to lead a person to Him. Paul reflects on those who were converted under his ministry. "For what is our hope or joy or crown of boasting before our Lord Jesus at his coming? Is it not you? For you are our glory and joy" (I Thess. 2:19, 20 R.S.V.). He calls the young Christians his "crown." In a wholesome sense, the boast of a Christian is those whom he has led to Christ. "He that winneth souls is wise" (Prov. 11:30). "And they that be wise shall shine as the brightness of the firmament; and they that turn many to righteousness as the stars forever and ever" (Dan. 12:3).

MAKING CONTACT
In Church
The teacher who loves people and is concerned for their eternal welfare will contact class members about salvation. Church educational organizations usually have a number of unsaved participants. The leader or teacher must be alert to the presence of the lost in his class and make an active effort to reach them. Some of these come from good Christian homes. The teacher should never take a student's salvation for granted but endeavor to speak to every individual in his class about salvation. Some who are thought to be Christians might not be. The opportunity to accept Christ as Savior must be given to each one.

At Home
Another place to seek lost people is in the home. The church leader often can make contact in the home (see chapters 9 and 10 on visitation) and thus enlarge his class and witness through reaching unchurched pupils. The teacher should be capable of engaging in personal conversation about salvation. Results may come instantaneously or take years. Some must learn and understand the

basic truths of Scripture before they can make an honest and sure decision, others respond to Christ immediately. A home visit which brings people in contact with church educational agencies can be a definite move toward evangelism.

KNOWING THE MESSAGE

Salvation is More Than Good Works

"For by grace are ye saved through faith; and that not of yourselves: it is the gift of God: not of works, lest any man should boast" (Eph. 2:8, 9). Salvation is all of Christ and the message of the New Testament is of grace, free from good works.

While all men should live better lives, this is not God's primary message to the lost. Most people already know they should live better lives for they get this message from many sources. However, they do not know how or even what is a better life. The teacher-evangelist presents the way to eternal life which results in better living. "But as many as received him, to them gave he power to become the sons of God, even to them that believe on his name" (Jn. 1:12). Only as people relate to God and have a new nature can they have better lives.

Salvation is More Than Reform

Reformation is good, but will not get a man to heaven. There are good reasons why a person evangelizing should not exhort the lost to reform. Man without Jesus Christ is a slave of sin and helpless to change. He cannot turn from sin to serve God. Only after Christ is received can the sinner follow God's commandments. "But God be thanked, that ye were the servants of sin, but ye have obeyed from the heart" (Rom. 6:17). Telling the lost to reform is like telling slaves to act like free men. They need more than a pronouncement; they need a deliverer.

To reform outward actions for a little while may result in the latter end being worse than the beginning. Jesus tells the parable of the man who swept his house, cleansed it, and cast out the evil spirit. Because the man did not fill the house, the evil spirit brought back seven other spirits more wicked than himself. And Jesus said, "The last state of that man is worse than the first" (Matt. 12:45). If an unsaved man does reform and change his living, he may feel that he has done God a favor and so deserves salvation. However, reformation is no substitute for redemption. True reformation, however, is to turn first to Christ who can change lives and then turn from sins (I Thess. 1:9).

Salvation is More Than Church Membership

One of the main motivations for getting people into the church is to get them under the sound of the gospel. Ultimately, it is felt, they will be converted. However, some people substitute church membership for salvation. Church membership can be a false security, making the unsaved feel he is right with God. An evangelist once said, "Hell will be full of unsaved church members."

Satan is anxious to sow tares among the wheat (Matt. 13:39) by getting unsaved into the church. This way he can introduce trouble and discredit the testimony of Christ. Since the church is the body of Christ (Eph. 1:22, 23), those who join should be those who are in Christ.

Nevertheless, unsaved should be invited to church services. Some people are converted by visiting the services of the church and hearing the gospel (I Cor. 14:23-25). When they come under the sound of the gospel they realistically face the claims of Christ. Paul testifies, "The gospel . . . is the power of God unto salvation to everyone that believeth" (Rom. 1:16).

PRESENTING THE MESSAGE

One must be sensitive to the leading of the Holy Spirit. The Holy Spirit will guide the teacher to the unsaved person, and then He will guide in what words to speak. The teacher who would evangelize must be careful not to offend and not to force a decision but patiently wait. He also must be careful not to substitute procrastination for patient waiting. It is often a mistake to put off speaking to a pupil assuming there is always another week. Procrastination can be just as harmful as tactless blundering.

The Message

Salvation is sometimes pictured as a road. "Enter ye in at the strait gate: for wide is the gate, and broad is the way, that leadeth to destruction, and many there be which go in thereat: Because strait is the gate, and narrow the way, which leadeth unto life" (Matt. 7:13, 14). In the book of Acts early Christianity was referred to as "the way" (Acts 9:2).

Man must follow God's road to heaven, just as the travelers followed the Roman roads during the time of Christ. Some have used the term "Roman Road to Salvation" in reference to the following verses to illustrate this fact. Also, the term is used because the verses used are chosen from one book in the Bible, Paul's Epistle to the Romans.

There are many other verses that could be used, and their inclusion by the teacher is encouraged. However, if a person who is not familiar with the Bible has his attention centered in only one book of the sixty-six in the Bible, he is less likely to become confused. Also, if only a few verses are explained well rather than many simply read, the honest seeker will more likely see God's plan of salvation.

The teacher might underline these four verses in his Bible and, more important, commit them to memory.

Romans 3:23	— Man's need
Romans 6:23	— Sin's penalty
Romans 5:8	— God's provision
Romans 10:9, 10	— Man's response

This outline has been so widely used that the original source is not known. Its wide use shows its effectiveness.[1]

Getting Started

Many people do not witness because they do not know how to start. One way to begin is for a teacher to share what Christ has done for him and what Christ means to him. His experience is one fact people can't refute. When Peter and John stood before the Sanhedrin, they shared what God had done for them. "For we cannot but speak the things which we have seen and heard" (Acts 4:20). Also, the healed man standing with them gave authority to their witness, "And beholding the man which was healed standing with them, they could say nothing against it" (Acts 4:14).

A testimony is simply telling what Christ means to a person. It might include the following:

How the need for salvation was recognized.

The facts of conversion experience.

What Christ means to him now.

Perhaps some cannot recall a definite time of salvation because they were converted early in life. However, they can share the reality of Christ now.

After a testimony, one of the following questions will help keep the conversation centered on spiritual matters.

"Would you like to know how you can meet Jesus Christ?"

"What is your reaction to that?"

"May I show you four verses in the Bible that explain how to secure eternal life?"

Clarifying the Way

At times the teacher has the joy of explaining salvation to a person who is ready to receive Christ. Following a Sunday school lesson or sermon by the pastor a person comes seeking salvation. In this event, a testimony is not needed to motivate a person to seek salvation. He is already motivated; hence, refer this person to Romans 3:23.

> ### Man's Need
> For all have sinned, and come short of the glory of God. Romans 3:23

The word "all" should be pointed out to include every human of all ages. The teacher should quickly clarify that he, also, is included. Even though he is a Christian he, too, has sinned. If the person has heard the Word of God properly taught, he will realize he has sinned (I Jn. 1:8, 10).

The teacher might point out that sin is breaking God's commandments as expressed in the Bible. However, if the person will not accept the fact he is a sinner, it may be useless to continue. A teacher once wisely said, "You can't get people converted till you get them lost." He meant a person must be convinced of his need for salvation before he truly seeks God.

> ### Sin's Penalty
> For the wages of sin is death; but the gift of God is eternal life through Jesus Christ our Lord.
> Romans 6:23

Because man has sinned, he must pay the penalty. Wages refers to that which is paid for work or labor. Wages, in everyday language, is that which a person has coming to him. This verse then means that all have death coming because they are sinners. Death is the salary paid by sin.

Note the contrast between a gift which is free and undeserved and wages which are paid for service. One works for sins and automatically gets death. Yet in contrast, God gives life as a gift. The term implies something that isn't deserved or expected. A gift usually is bestowed by someone who cares. God has given eternal life through Jesus Christ, but sin can only lead to death.

> ### God's Provision
> But God commendeth his love toward us, in that, while we were yet sinners, Christ died for us.
> Romans 5:8

The gospel is good news — Christ died for sinners. "The wages of sin is death," but Christ died in man's stead. He died in place of the sinner. The sinner should have received the punishment, but Christ took his place. Christ received the sinner's death and the sinner, Christ's life. This is the proof of Christ's love. Many understand the events that surround the cross. The meaning of the cross with Christ, our substitute, is the basic communication that is necessary here.

> ### Man's Response
> That if thou shalt confess with thy mouth the Lord Jesus, and shalt believe in thine heart that God hath raised him from the dead, thou shalt be saved.
>
> Romans 10:9

There are many people who intellectually know that Christ died, and some of these even say, "Christ died for me." But, if they do not make a personal response, they are not saved.

In the picture of a Roman road, the road now branches. One branch is broad and leads to destruction. The other road is narrow and leads to eternal life. The person must make a choice. He should be given the opportunity to receive Christ and be shown the importance of a decision.

The person must believe in his heart. This is foundational. He also must confess Christ. The R.S.V. translates this verse to read that he must confess "Jesus is Lord." This is giving special place to Christ in the life.

Believe has various meanings. Believe can mean speculation. "I believe it is going to rain tomorrow." Believe can be acceptance of fact. "I believe in the historical fact of the Revolutionary War." Some have knowledge of the historical fact of the life of Jesus but this knowledge won't convert them, "the devils also believe, and tremble" (James 2:19). Believe can be accepting and acting upon a truth. This is the belief that converts.

Belief that accepts and acts upon truth results in receiving Jesus Christ as Savior. "But as many as received him, to them gave he power to become the sons of God" (Jn. 1:12).

Bringing to Decision

After an explanation of salvation, a person should not be left with a head knowledge. An opportunity for decision should be given.

Some of the following might be used as a transition from verse explanation to getting the person to make a volitional choice:

"Do you understand God's plan of salvation?"

"Would you like to have eternal life?"

"Why don't we pray and you receive Christ now?"

If the person gives an affirmative answer, encourage him to pray himself. The Bible nowhere says that a person must pray to be converted; however, prayer is a good way to approach God for salvation.

Instruct the person to pray simply and ask Christ to come into his life. He doesn't need an elaborate petition, nor does it have to be a long prayer. Just a sincere prayer. Suggest to him that he just tell God what he has told the teacher. Some encouragement like the following may help:

"Do you want to receive Christ? – tell God."

"Do you want to be rid of sin? – tell God."

"Prayer is talking to God like you are talking to me."

After the person has received Christ, the teacher might offer a prayer of thanksgiving. The prayer should be short and to the point.

SUMMARY

What does a person need to know for salvation? First, the individual must know and acknowledge that he is a sinner. There must be conviction of sin and a knowledge that he must turn from it. Second, the individual must recognize the penalty for his sins, which is death. Third, the individual must realize that Jesus Christ died for his sins. The good news is that Jesus paid the price as his substitute on the cross. And finally, he should know that if Christ is received as Savior from sin, He will forgive. But He must be accepted by faith which is casting and resting of oneself on Christ.

NOTES

1. The Four Spiritual Laws also have been used effectively. A small pamphlet, "Have You Heard of the Four Spiritual Laws?", by William R. Bright, is available from Campus Crusade for Christ, Arrowhead Springs, San Bernardino, Calif. 92403.

REVIEW QUESTIONS

1. Why should the opportunity to accept Christ be given to each class member?
2. What is the relationship of salvation and church membership?
3. What four verses from the book of Romans summarize the way of salvation?
4. How does a testimony often pave the way for explaining salvation?
5. What is the place of prayer in salvation?

FOR DISCUSSION AND APPLICATION

1. List the people you know who attended church regularly before accepting Christ. What does this show regarding the place of church educational agencies in salvation?
2. Imagine you are at a family reunion and an unsaved relative begins to criticize the church for its failures and you for teaching Sunday school. How would you lead the conversation to a discussion of his need for Christ?
3. Consider yourself a teacher who has just been asked, "How can I accept Christ?" Clearly explain how.

BIBLIOGRAPHY

Downey, M. W. **The Art of Soul-Winning.** Grand Rapids: Baker Book House, 1957.

Harrison, Eugene M. **How to Win Souls.** Wheaton, Ill.: Van Kampen Press, 1952.

Hyles, Jack. **Let's Go Soul Winning.** Murfreesboro, Tenn.: Sword of the Lord Publishers, 1962.

Little, Paul. **How to Give Away Your Faith.** Chicago: Moody Press, 1966.

Lovett, C. S. **Soul Winning Classes Made Easy.** Baldwin Park, Calif.: Personal Christianity, 1962.

CHAPTER SIX

EVANGELISM OF CHILDREN

How long should you wait before trying to lead the new child in your Sunday school class to Christ?

If you teach nursery children, how can you be evangelistic?

How might you tell a child the story of salvation by using the fingers of your hand?

Children have many problems which are barriers to salvation. They need teachers ready to give Christian guidance. And, more important, those who are able to lead them to Christ. The Lord loved children for He said, "Suffer little children to come unto me, and forbid them not: for of such is the kingdom of God" (Lk. 18: 16). Those who love children as Jesus did will bring them to the Savior.

CHILDREN NEED CHRIST

A child is capable of accepting Christ or rejecting Him. Children, like adults who know not Christ, naturally choose evil and turn from God. It is not easy for them to disregard the many wrong influences which clamor for their attention and interest. As these sinful attractions on children are recognized, the importance of evangelism becomes more apparent.

To counteract the pull of sin, children need their parents' companionship during the crucial years of childhood. They need love and security. They need care and discipline. They need the influence of godly parents. But they often lack Christian conversation, Christian literature, and Christian teaching in their homes and so become dependent upon the church to tell them of Christ.

THE IMPORTANCE OF WINNING CHILDREN

When the disciples discouraged the bringing of children to Jesus, He rebuked them and encouraged children to come (Mark 10:14).

Matthew 18:1-14 emphasizes the evangelism of children. Children are given as examples of humility. They are not to be offended (v. 6), are not to be despised (v. 10), and it is the will of the Father that they not perish (v. 14).

The young child who is won to the Lord has a total life potential to be used in God's service. Not only is a soul saved but a life of service to God and man is conserved. Gypsy Smith said in regard to the salvation of children, "You save an old man you save a unit but save a boy and you have a multiplication table."[1]

Another evangelist was asked how many people received Christ in a meeting. "Three and a half," was his reply. "Oh, you mean three adults and one child," was the response. "No, three children and one adult. For the child has his whole life before him, the adult only has half a life left."

Many homes have a growing child with all the potentials for good or evil. He must be given an opportunity to accept the Lord. If the church educational program has an active program to reach children for Christ, the home as well as the child is helped. The church that takes time for children will usually find a home that has time for the church.

GROUPING FOR EVANGELISM

Often the question is raised, "At what age is a child able to accept Jesus as Savior?" This varies from child to child. The Word of God teaches that children can learn about God, Jesus Christ, and other foundational truths while young. "That from a child thou hast known the Holy Scriptures, which are able to make thee wise unto salvation through faith which is in Christ Jesus" (II Tim. 3:15). So children must be exposed to the message of God's Word, and taught that God is love. They must be taught that man is by nature a sinner and predisposed to turn away from God. They must be taught that God is holy and cannot accept sinful things. By such teaching, the child is being nurtured to respond to the claims of Christ during his youth.

Some influences which prepare a child to accept Jesus are worship periods, Bible reading, conversations about spiritual things, prayer, and singing of Christian songs both at church and home. Also, the radiant and godly life of the teacher exerts an influence. They may not remember all that is said, but they will never forget your friendliness.

The best time to bring a child to the Lord is when he is prepared by the Holy Spirit and ready. The teacher must pray that the Holy Spirit will make him sensitive to a child's need and prepare the child's heart to respond to the gospel. An alertness to the time when a child becomes conscious of sin and feels his need of coming to the Lord should characterize every Christian teacher. A child's decision should be recognized even though he previously made one. God's working in the heart is not limited to a teacher's plan.

Church educational programs are often graded by ages so that pupils' needs are similar and better teaching results. Evangelism is another good reason for age grouping. Evangelistic emphasis can be more effective when geared to those of the same age group.

The cradle roll (*birth to 2*) provides an organized outreach of the Sunday school into homes where there are new babies. Each year many parents in a community can be reached with the gospel through an organized cradle roll program. It is an opportunity to reach a home that is ready for the gospel because of hearts warmed by the experience of new life.

Gear *the nursery* (*age 2-3*) to evangelism. The nursery has a ministry to the child. The child learns that the church is God's house, God loves him, the Bible tells him of God, and he is to love God. These are tremendous concepts that can be learned early in life and which prepare the child for a salvation experience. The nursery has a further evangelistic contribution. Many fathers and mothers will attend a Sunday school or church where there are facilities for their children. They are more likely to respond to the gospel when they can listen to a sermon without the interruptions of a small child.

Kindergartners (*age 4-5*) are at an important age. Some people believe they are too young to be converted. Others feel that kindergarten children can know they do wrong and that when a person realizes he sins, he is old enough to receive Christ. The teacher must be careful to be led of the Spirit in personally dealing with children about salvation. Don't minimize the response of small children. A display of faith by the small child is great in God's sight. Because some come from Bible-teaching homes, they are aware of God. Others have no concept of God in their lives. All are old enough to love God, pray to God and, in their own way, serve God.

Primary children (*age 6-8*) can place their faith in Christ. They realize that they have sinned and often are ready to respond to the gospel. Small children find it easy and natural to trust Jesus as Savior. For those who do not experience conversion at this time, the primary years can be a time to lay vital groundwork that will lead to a knowledge and conviction of sin and ultimately to personal acceptance of Jesus Christ.

Many feel that *junior age* (*age 9-11*) is the best age for evangelism. Surely most have an awareness of accountability and recognize a need to respond to the gospel. The Sunday school teacher must present an evangelistic challenge to the junior if he is to fulfill one of the greatest responsibilities of teaching this age. The teacher should guard against pushing children into church membership or baptism. They may need considerable instruction not being fully aware of the meaning of some of the obligations nor prepared for the responsibilities.

PRESENTING THE GOSPEL

Presenting the gospel to children takes prayerful preparation and thoughtful expression. Children should not be expected to apply to their hearts a truth which the teacher has not applied to his own life. It is difficult for a child to get any closer to the Lord in his experience than his teacher.

In presenting the gospel to children, language must be simple and on the level of the child. Theological or biblical words should not be taken for granted but explained plainly. Many Sunday school manuals provide a glossary of terms graded to the understanding of the child. These can be helpful to a teacher. Some modern translations and paraphrases which attempt to place gospel truth in easily understood terms are often useful in teaching children. Unclear terms often must be explained many times. Some words or expressions that are difficult for children are sin, everlasting life, saved, died for our sins, receive or accept Christ as Savior, sinner, forgiveness, God's love. The fundamental facts that explain the gospel are:

- God loves you (Jn. 3:16)
- All have sinned (Rom. 3:23)
- Christ died to pay for your sin (I Cor. 15:3)
- Believe Christ died for your sin (Jn. 1:12)
- When you believe, you receive everlasting life (Rom. 6:23)

How to use these verses with the hand as an illustration will be explained later in this chapter.

The underlying motive and universal language which a child understands is love. When a teacher faces his class or an individual pupil, his non-verbal language must say, "I love you." His looks, actions, attitudes, and words must radiate love from the Lord. A knowledge of child psychology is helpful for a successful worker with children but there is no substitute for love.

PUBLIC INVITATIONS

There are dangers in giving a public invitation to children. Children are taught to be obedient to parents, so they may do what the "adult up front" asks of them. As a result, the decision may not be a spiritual reality. Also, children are influenced by others; they express a desire to be converted because their friends are doing so. They have tender hearts. Stories that play on the emotions may cause them to make an outward response, especially stories of danger, death, or loss of parents. The teacher must be careful that decisions made by children are properly motivated and are centered in faith in Christ.

When talking with children who respond in a general evangelistic meeting, it is necessary to determine the basis of their faith. Faith must be in Jesus Christ. Children can have a subjective faith that comes from desire, but which is not based on Christ. While this is not saving faith, it can provide an opportunity to make clear that trust must be in the Christ.

An open invitation in a Sunday school class is sometimes given simply because the teacher is hesitant to talk personally with his pupils about Christ. When a general invitation is given, the teacher should carefully plan to personally explain salvation to each child who responds. The best way may be to encourage children to come to the teacher after class or during an informal occasion such as a social time.

If the teacher must give a public invitation because the group is large and time doesn't permit a personal interview with all, children can be prepared by having them bow their heads and close their eyes. This can help assure a reverent atmosphere. The invitation should not be too easy or too difficult. If it has no meaning to the child, he might respond without change of heart. If the invitation is too difficult, the timid child might be discouraged. Decisions should not be forced upon children. A child's reticence may be because he does not understand what the teacher is saying, or he may not be ready at the moment. It is not necessary to wait until the end of a lesson to extend an invitation. Occasionally, a teacher might pause in the middle of the lesson and invite children to accept the Lord Jesus Christ. The guidance of the Holy Spirit is available to those who seek and will follow it. A teacher should never permit the amount of lesson material to prevent him from taking the necessary time for an invitation to accept Christ. Lessons are taught to change lives, not just to communicate content.

PERSONALLY EXPLAINING THE WAY

There are a number of ways and Scripture verses which may be used when leading a child to the Lord. The following method uses John 3:16 as a basis for explaining the way of salvation. There are five simple divisions in John 3:16 which are as follows: (1) God so loved, (2) the world, (3) that he gave His only begotten Son, (4) that whosoever believeth in Him, (5) should not perish but have everlasting life. A simple plan is to let each finger on a hand represent one part of God's great plan of salvation.[2]

In the center of God's plan is His love so the middle finger can stand for God's love. God created all things. He made the beautiful flowers and trees, the birds and bees buzzing in the trees, the animals, and grass all around. The sun, the moon, and stars also were made by Him. And He made each boy, girl, man, and woman. He loves each one.

The index finger can represent the world. Each child is one of the people in the world. The teacher should be specific and personal here. The child does not belong to God because he is a sinner. He is separated from God because of sin in the heart. God is holy and cannot look at sin. "All have sinned and come short of the glory of God" (Rom. 3:23). This sin must be forgiven before a child can become a child of God.

The thumb can stand for the Son, the Lord Jesus Christ. Jesus is God's Son. God sent His Son to die on the cross for man's sin. Christ had no sin, but He paid for sin on the cross. Man deserves to die, but Jesus died instead. But He did not stay dead. He rose again from the dead after three days. He showed Himself to His friends and they were glad. Jesus is now alive. He is in heaven. He talks to the Heavenly Father about believers. He is waiting for each child to make Him his Friend and Savior.

The ring finger can stand for the sinner who receives Jesus Christ. When a person receives Jesus Christ as Savior, he is saved. He must believe that He died in his place and trust Him to forgive. A brief prayer such as "Dear Lord Jesus, I know I am a sinner, I now believe in you and accept you as my Savior. Forgive my sins and make me your own" is often the turning point from darkness to light.

Finally, the little finger can stand for the assurance that God has given eternal life. Using John 3:16 or Romans 6:23 a child who has received Christ can be shown that he now has eternal life, not because the teacher said so, but because God's Word says so, ". . . whosoever (pupil) believeth in Christ . . . hath everlasting life" (Jn. 3:16). This eternal life is a gift from God not because the child prayed for it, but God gave it in response to his faith.

If the child is older, he will be able to understand how the thumb helps pick up objects. In a similar way, Christ helps believers live the Christian life. As the teacher touches the thumb to the middle finger he might discuss the expression of love. When he touches it to the index finger, he discusses the giving of Christ's life for the world. By touching the ring finger he pictures the giving of life to those who believe. As he touches the thumb to the little finger, he discusses how eternal life is provided through Christ.[3]

AFTER THE CHILD RECEIVES CHRIST

After a child has asked Christ to come into his life, a prayer of thanksgiving for salvation should be offered audibly by both child and teacher. Encourage the pupil to tell someone of his decision as soon as possible. If the child accepted Christ privately in church, let him tell the pastor, or his class. If public invitations are given in church, it is good to encourage the child to go forward confessing that Christ is his Savior. Make sure he shares his experience with his parents. If the parents are not Christians, the teacher may go home with the child or call during the week to help explain what has happened.

A good teacher will guide the child in spiritual growth, encouraging him, and praying with him. He should be enrolled in church activities and introduced to mature Christians in the church who can encourage him in his Christian walk. This added Christian fellowship will strengthen his Christian life.

The child must be told the importance of prayer. He should understand that prayer is talking to God. Since prayer, like breathing, must be regular, he should be encouraged to practice daily prayer of thanksgiving for guidance and help from temptation. Opportunity for prayer also should be provided in the various educational agencies of the church.

The child also must be taught the importance of Bible reading. Every child should have a Bible and a reading guide which he can follow. Cooperation with the pastor in suggesting materials to be used can aid in establishing a church reading program for all members.

Witnessing also is essential for Christian growth. If a child is taught how to win others, it will become much easier to witness later as a youth or adult. Sometimes the Wordless Book, which uses different colored pages to depict the steps to salvation, can be used by a youngster. The simple faith and trust of a child can be shared with his classmates at school and his companions in the neighborhood.

SUMMARY

The teacher-evangelist has a great responsibility. He must teach the lesson faithfully, and know each child in his class well. This will help him to be ready when the Holy Spirit prompts him to speak to a child about accepting the Lord Jesus Christ. He must know how to lead a child to Christ and be ready to respond to the child's sincere questions about eternal matters. Once a decision is made, the teacher becomes a guide to spiritual development so that the one who confesses Christ can grow to spiritual maturity.

NOTES

1. David M. Dawson, **More Power in Soul Winning** (Grand Rapids: Zondervan Publishing House, 1947), p. 58. Quoted from Gypsy Smith.
2. The idea for using the hand came from Walter H. Werner, "How to Lead a Child to Christ," **Guidelines for Christian Parents** (Lincoln, Neb.: Good News Broadcasting Assn., Inc., 1967), pp. 12-16.
3. A helpful booklet, written by Joyce Gibson, which can be used in explaining salvation to juniors is **For People's Sake** (Wheaton, Ill.: Scripture Press, 1969). Additional helpful information on how to lead children to Christ can be found in Dr. Mary E. LeBar's book, **Living in God's Family** (Wheaton, Ill.: Scripture Press, 1957).

REVIEW QUESTIONS

1. What biblical basis is there for evangelism among young children?
2. How does dividing children by age help in evangelism?
3. What dangers should be avoided in a public invitation to children to accept Christ?
4. In what ways can a teacher give opportunity to receive Christ during a lesson period?
5. What are some ways to keep in contact with a child who has accepted Christ?

FOR DISCUSSION AND APPLICATION

1. Interview a church teacher of children and ask three questions.
   (1) At what age are children usually brought to Christ in your work?
   (2) How do you lead a child to Christ?
   (3) How are children followed up after they have made a decision for Christ?
2. Request the opportunity of bringing a brief evangelistic story to one of the early childhood departments. Discuss with classmates how you should move from the facts of the story to decision by the children.
3. Prepare a file of materials which might be used in evangelism of children. Include such items as the Wordless Book, children's tracts, lists of available films for children, devotional aids for children.

BIBLIOGRAPHY

Dobbins, Gaines S. **Winning the Children.** Nashville: Broadman Press, 1953.

Coleman, Frank C. **The Romance of Winning Children.** Cleveland: Union Gospel Press, 1948.

LeBar, Lois. **Children in the Bible School.** Westwood, N.J.: Fleming H. Revell Co., 1952.

Soderholm, Marjorie. **Explaining Salvation to Children: Helping a Child Receive Christ as Savior.** Minneapolis: Beacon Publishers, 1962.

EVANGELISM OF YOUTH

Do you recognize the many changes in an adolescent's life?
Could you help a youth answer, "Who am I?"
Can you tell a young person how to accept Christ?

The vast potential and the unique problems locked up in youth challenge every church teacher. Adolescent years are the years of decision. The span of time from the age of twelve through twenty-four is a comparatively small portion of the total life expectancy but this is a time when many accept the Lord. Although adolescence is a period of honest doubts and honest questions, teens are spiritually sensitive and religious awakening is evident.

RESPONSIVENESS TO LOVE

Many movements challenge youth. Whether distorted or commendable, these require dedication and sacrifice. If youth can give themselves for these, surely they can give themselves to Christ and the challenge of obedience to Him.

At times youth seem to have a cynical attitude toward life. However, this is only a veneer. Underneath is a tenderness to life and a need for love which only Christ can provide. In the record of the conversation between Jesus and the rich young man, Mark comments on the fact that "Jesus . . . loved him" (Mark 10: 21). Christ's attitude toward all youth in all generations is love. If we are going to reach young people, we also must love them. At times it is difficult for adults to love youth for teens frustrate or seem to threaten them. As long as the adults in a group outnumber the young people present and thus maintain control, there is no problem. But when youth outnumber adults many older persons forget love, and barriers arise which become hindrances to witness for Christ.

CONFLICTING ETHICAL CUSTOMS

Young people represent a restless and troublesome segment of our society. Today's young people are caught in the midst of pressures. On one side they face pressure from their teen companions, on the other from adults. There is tension between peer demands and church doctrines. Conflicting demands bombard youth. The result is rebellion and conflict.

The adolescent is in a no-man's-land — a buffer zone between childhood and adulthood. He wants to be treated as a mature person. He does not want others to decide for him but wants to find out for himself. However, he lacks the judgment and insight of adulthood. He does not understand his own behavior and is unable to predict his own conduct. It is this young person, who faces pressures from the outside as well as pressures from within, who needs Christ.

A CHANGING AGE

Physical Change

In early teens a physical change introduces adolescence. Teens enter a new experience. The physical change of puberty usually takes approximately thirteen months. Although today's teens go through puberty earlier than did their parents, this period of the half-child/half-adult often is extended into high school. During puberty, the skeletal frame grows and an adolescent's interest in sex becomes active.

Social Change

Society has pushed children to grow up. They are encouraged to date before they are ready and act like adults while still children. Perhaps the title of an article in a popular women's magazine is a fitting commentary on these changing times, "Mascara on My Lollipop." Social pressure has resulted in problems for youth which can best be faced with a sense of security and inner spiritual stability.

Psychological Change

During this period there is a new interest in physical appearance. Prior to this they had little thought of their appearance. This self-awareness comes suddenly. "Am I normal?" the teen may ask. "What's happening to me?" Sometimes these physical changes trigger psychological problems. How teens think they look and how they feel about their looks are important and affect their attitudes and relationships.

They must understand that their physical form and development come from God. Scriptural attitudes concerning their bodies must be presented. They should be made aware that God wants their bodies to be used for worship and service.

Intellectual Change

Youth is the age of doubts. These generally center about self, God, and family. Why do they doubt? Their self-awareness is focusing for the first time in life. Without a variety of experiences to temper them, they tend to be idealistic. Teen-agers often expect the best, the ultimate, and the perfect. So they are critical. However, critical thinking can lead to creative thinking and must be guided by the dedicated teacher to thoughtful consideration of life.

Habit Change

Youth styles and fads change. They intend to create a world all their own. Most teens fall into line with fads to symbolize their identity with their youth sub-culture. To others, fads are a way to rebel against adult authority. Fighting teen fads may hinder communication and opportunity for witness. Unless they are immoral, most fads can be ignored. The gulf between youth and adult worlds, while not created by the teacher, must be bridged by him if he is to reach young people. He must provide a ministry that is definitely pointed at the conversion experience even if indirect in message. The teacher must always be ready to give information, interpretation, and example, so as to help develop Christian attitudes.

"WHO AM I?" — STEPPING STONE TO CONVERSION

Youth is seeking identity. "Who am I?" is the inner question of the young person. In the past few years, there has been a rising emphasis on self-identification psychology. Psychologists are finding that youth goes through an identity crisis as he develops. Identity is a quest among youth. They want to be accepted as persons. They are bombarded with the "Who am I?" question at school, in teen literature, and other forms of media. The Bible has an answer for this and the evangelist can move from the self-identity need into communication of the gospel.

A Sinner

Whether subjectively felt or not, youth is a sinner. This sinful nature must be viewed and interpreted for what it is — rebellion against God. In seeing himself as a sinner, youth is on the road to understanding salvation.

A Loved Individual

No single additional factor can contribute so much to his sense of self-esteem as to be loved unconditionally (Jn. 3:16). God in love has a plan for each life which is in the best interest of that person, and in love He will enable a young person to fulfill that plan.

A Deciding Person

During childhood most major decisions were made for him. As he approaches the end of adolescence, he must choose a mate, a career, and a role in life which will bring personal satisfaction. But he alone must make these choices. To choose too early is to run the risk of a detoured life. To choose too late is to run the danger of missing God's best. Youth desire to be self-determining individuals. They demand the right to choose their own clothes, their own friends, and their own means of happiness. Their greatest choice concerns heaven and hell. They must make that choice for themselves. However, in this grave responsibility of choice between life and death, young people need a mature teacher-evangelist to guide them, to answer honestly their honest doubts, and to lead them to right decisions by accepting the Lord Jesus Christ as Savior and Lord. As Joshua challenged his hearers, "Choose you this day whom ye will serve . . ." (Josh. 24:15), the teacher-evangelist has a solemn responsibility to present youth with the challenge of salvation.

An Accepted Person

Teens are concerned about being accepted by peers and adults. They also should be concerned about being "accepted in the beloved" (Eph. 1:6). Teens should realize, "I am one who has been accepted by God, because I know Jesus Christ." The teacher must face youth with the obligation of responding to God's provision of salvation before they can be accepted.

Each young person must make meaningful relationships, for the depth of life's meaning is found in friends. If they will become friends with Christ and receive Him, they will establish a relationship with God. Then they can branch out into in-depth relationships with other members of God's family.

Christian youth need not remain with their conflicts indefinitely unresolved. While it is true no one can extricate himself from sin and problems, yet God, through the Holy Spirit, can and does for the new birth produces a transformed nature.

The teacher-evangelist must recognize teen-age doubts and build a ministry on an intelligent interpretation of the Bible. The teacher should never laugh at their questions, but teach them the difference between criticism and evaluation. When they ask questions a teacher can't answer, he must be willing to say, "I don't know." Youth won't listen to a teacher who thinks he knows everything.

One of the ways in which youth can find answers to their problems is through Bible study. Here they find the answer to life's need — the Lord Jesus Christ. The lives of young people can be changed if they learn to dig intelligently, thoroughly, and systematically into the Word of God.

EVANGELIZING THROUGH BIBLE STUDY

Assumptions

The Word of God is the final authority. It is revelation from

God that demands a response. Therefore, the teacher must teach for a decision and seek for teens to respond to the Word. Teenagers should realize that God's Word is not optional, it is essential. The Bible brings conviction of sin and leads to transformation of life. Therefore, Bible study is basic for evangelism.

Attitudes

The whole Bible must be taught to apply to the whole life. Bible study can be meaningful and purposeful only when directed to the life of the students.

All of life is sacred in the sense that Christ is to be at the center. The Bible has principles for all of life and should be related to every need. The Word of God is truth. "Thy Word is truth" (Jn. 17:17), our Lord asserted. So life must be molded according to the Word of God.

Approach

The task of the teacher-evangelist is to guide youth in exploring the Scriptures. Young people should bring the Bible with them to church because it is used in class. Direct involvement is a necessity in Bible teaching. Teaching can be just as evangelistic as a preaching service. Any method that brings lost teens into contact with the message of the Scriptures is evangelistic. A direct study of the Bible is a vital element in all successful evangelistic teaching.

Participation in Bible study involves mental and emotional responses. Since youth have the capacity for critical thinking, every session of the class should be thought provoking. There is no need to resort to sensationalism or startling remarks in order to get youth to think, for nothing is more powerful than an idea. Learning takes place when a student is actively engaged in considering, discussing, analyzing, interpreting, and applying ideas to meet a need in the life. In so doing, youth are not only learning facts, but they are building up intellectual and emotional attitudes which will become a foundation for decision for Christ.

Atmosphere

Teaching is most effective when there is participation. In an informal situation, the teacher can make it possible for any class member to ask questions and to become involved in the teaching-learning situation. The teacher must welcome questions from the students. A question may be the one thing keeping youth from accepting Christ. Questions are evidence of interest. Therefore, they should be answered from the Word. The true teacher will join the youth in the quest for truth. A willingness to learn with the student will prove to be a great asset in motivating the young person to receive Jesus Christ.

Classroom chairs may be arranged around a table in conference style for smaller classes. Discussion is easier when students face each other. The table is handy for an open Bible and other books. Writing paper and pencils may be used. Other arrangements may be necessary for larger groups. The classroom arrangement is important for the involvement in a learning situation can contribute to the acceptance or rejection of an evangelistic appeal.

Each student should have his own Bible and be given opportunity to become familiar with it through use. At times silent reading of assigned passages, or guided search for Bible answers to class questions can direct attention to salvation.

The teacher can maintain a high interest level in searching the Scriptures by making resources known. Books in the church library can provide help. People within the congregation are often available for information youth need. Youth who feel at liberty to discuss temporal problems with teacher and pastor also will be free to share their spiritual questions with them.

BRINGING YOUTH TO DECISION

"Reaching youth in time provides them with firm anchorage and steady rudder."[1] There needs to be a crisis experience in the young person's life when he comes to the realization he is a rebel against God. C. S. Norberg expresses this realization of rebellion strongly, "There must be a sin-experience, sin-feeling, sin-despair, and sin-deliverance."[2]

As presented in the book of Romans, the teacher must explain the need of salvation (Rom. 3:23), the penalty of sin (Rom. 6: 23), God's provision (Rom. 5:8), and the necessity of man's response (Rom. 10:9, 10).

It must be made clear to the young person that conversion is an experience which includes the three elements in his personality. Conversion includes a voluntary turning away from sin. The negative aspect, repentance, involves:

1. An intellectual element: a recognition of sin as the individual's personal sin and rebellion (Ps. 51:3, 7, 11).
2. An emotional element: change of feeling, a heart sorrow for sin, and love for God.
3. A volitional element: inward turning from sin, a renunciation of sin and sinful ways (Ps. 51:5, 7, 10; Jer. 25:5).

Conversion also involves faith which is a voluntary change in the sinner in which he turns to Christ. It involves:

1. An intellectual element: acceptance of the Scriptures and what it teaches about the provision of Christ's death on the cross.

2. An emotional element: a personal assent to the power and grace of God as revealed in Christ Jesus, and trusting Him as the only Savior from sin.

3. A volitional element: a dedication of the soul to Christ and a positive act of receiving and appropriating Christ as the only source of pardon and spiritual life.[3]

AFTER YOUTH ACCEPT CHRIST

Youth need to be evangelized and youth need to be involved in evangelism. A Christian teen needs to be grounded in the Word of God if he is to mature. Some will accept Christ and return to a home which knows nothing of Christ. Church leaders will need to assume some responsibility in nurturing this young person and grounding him in the Word. Chapter eleven will be helpful in this.

"One of the best ways to win youth to the Lord is through the witness of Christian teens."[4] Youth should be involved in the church's evangelistic thrust. Thirty-four different activities which can challenge youth are suggested by the Simpsons. Some of these are:

Canvassing	Prayer cells	Campus forums
Traveling choirs	Billboard posters	Literature distribution
Gospel films	After-game socials	Hobby or craft clubs[5]
Vacation evangelism		

Gunnar Hoglund suggests eleven different approaches to reach non-church youth. Some of these include:

Mail evangelism	Telephone brigades	Evangelistic crusades
Athleetic missions	Resort evangelism	Coffee house evangelism[6]

Youth have been challenged to prepare then teach vacation Bible schools during the summer. They have also been challenged to prepare and then teach five-day backyard Bible clubs. Youth will respond to a challenge.

SUMMARY

Leading young people to Christ is a privilege and obligation. A young person thus won to Christ has a foundation for right living and a set of goals for which to strive. The teacher can help settle their convictions and loyalties and guide them in life's quest. The church must reach, teach, and win youth to Christ. The church also must use youth to reach youth.

NOTES

1. Ted W. Engstrom, "All Out for Youth," **Moody Monthly**, LVII:25 (July, 1957).
2. Sverre Norberg, **The Varieties of Christian Experience** (Minneapolis: Augsburg Publishing House, 1937), p. 137.
3. Refer to Augustus Hopkins Strong, **Systematic Theology** (Westwood, N.J.: Fleming H. Revell Co., 1907), pp. 832-39.
4. Edward D. and Frances F. Simpson, "Evangelism of Youth" in Roy G. Irving and Roy B. Zuck (eds.), **Youth and the Church** (Chicago: Moody Press, 1969), p. 174.
5. **Ibid.**, p. 175.
6. Gunnar Hoglund, "Reaching Non-Church Youth," in **1969 Workshop Outlines** (Chicago: Greater Chicago Sunday School Assn., 1969), p. 5.

REVIEW QUESTIONS

1. In what ways is adolescence a changing age?
2. How does the Bible characterize youth?
3. How can Bible study contribute to youth evangelism?
4. Show how youth coming to a decision for Christ affects his intellect, emotion, and will.
5. List ways a converted youth can be helped to grow spiritually.

FOR DISCUSSION AND APPLICATION

1. Observe five teen-agers in your church or community and make anecdotal records of their actions in expressing self-identity, freedom, activity, and feelings. Endeavor to get one anecdote in each category for each student. A chart of findings might read as follows.

Student	Self-identity	Freedom	Activity	Feelings
Stephen	Wore mod clothes	Skipped school without explanation	Shot baskets for an hour	Argued strongly when his idea challenged

2. Some teen-agers have an early religious experience to look back upon but no confidence that they belong to God. Discuss various ways such a teen-ager might be helped spiritually.
3. Examine your church educational program to determine what it contributes to teen-age conversion and spiritual growth.

BIBLIOGRAPHY

Irving, Roy C. and Zuck, Roy B. **Youth and the Church.** Chicago: Moody Press, 1968.
Person, Peter P. **The Church and Modern Youth.** Grand Rapids: Zondervan Publishing House, 1963.
Ridenour, Fritz. **Tell It Like It Is.** Glendale, Calif.: Regal Press, 1968.
Tani, Henry. **Venture in Youth Work.** Philadelphia: Christian Education Press, 1957.
Towns, Elmer L. **Successful Youth Work.** Glendale, Calif.: Regal Press, 1966.

EVANGELISM
OF ADULTS

Can you explain the way of salvation to an adult?
Name the adults you know who have lost contact with the church?
Have you ever won an adult friend to Christ?

When God began the human race, he made adults. Although the Bible clearly shows God's interest in children, the great programs center around men and women. A small Samuel answered God's voice in the tabernacle and David defeated Goliath as a shepherd lad. But leadership in both Old and New Testaments rested with adults. Our Lord trained adult leaders who shaped the course of the world. Today, the divine imperative is for men and women, whose lives have been changed by the Lord, to reach lost adults for Christ.

ADULT NEEDS

While the primary need of adults is spiritual, there also are many personal needs in the adult world. An understanding of these will help in winning adults to Christ.

Relationship With God

Needs demand attention. Some are felt needs; for example, affection, self-respect, peer approval, independence, and commitment. Often adults can be reached through their felt needs. The adult will listen to the claims of Christ when he realizes God is interested in his problems. The acceptance of the gospel makes a difference in man's reaction to pressures. Although man is usually aware of felt needs, underneath is the spiritual need of which he may not be aware.

Adults need Christ and a proper relationship with Him. The adult should be guided into a meaningful understanding and appreciation of the teachings, life, and sacrifice of the Lord Jesus Christ. The adult should have an opportunity to accept Christ as Savior from sin, and the experience of commitment to Christ as Lord. He must also have a knowledge and an experience of the person and work of the Holy Spirit as teacher, guide, and source of power.

Recognition of Failure

Life may have regrets for adults. Certain goals set early in life have not been attained. A feeling of guilt may be present because they have not done the best for their children. Their conscience could be troubled because of wrongs that have never been rectified. Because of these failures, the adult may have an attitude of defeat, bitterness, and even cynicism.

Failures point up human frailty. They provide opportunity to guide men humbly to seek God. God allows some failures in order to reveal that He is faithful and just to forgive both the present and the past (I Jn. 1:9). Failures ultimately prove God's mercy. No one can relive the past. But God can forgive the past and man can take care of the present and the future by settling a transaction with God for salvation.

Strength for the Future

"As for man, his days are as grass: as a flower of the field, so he flourisheth . . . The wind passeth over it, and it is gone . . ." (Ps. 103:15, 16). Man knows the brevity of life. He is here to live for a few short years. During these years he is constantly faced with tomorrow. Decisions are made which will affect tomorrow. "Where will my employment take me?" "What will be the result of my latest opportunity of advancement?" "How will my children turn out?" Each of man's problems forces him to think of consequences.

The Bible deals with the past, present, and future. Christ will forgive the past when a person places faith in Him. The Bible provides many specific examples of how to face the present world. The adult must be led into the Bible for his answers. Biblical teaching about the future, its rewards and punishment in connection with life after death, must be clearly taught.

As the Bible is taught, more than factual presentation is needed. Teaching must be for decision, because man's dilemma demands an answer. To the unsaved the emphasis is NOW, "Now is the accepted time; . . . now is the day of salvation" (II Cor. 6:2). Salvation must be secured now in order to be secure after this life.

ADULT WORLD ENVIRONMENT

Adulthood usually comprises a span of fifty years or more. The cultural environment in which adults live needs to be appraised because it contains both assets and liabilities. The pressure is heavy upon adults. If we are to interest and reach adults, we must understand them and their world.

Mobility

Mobility has accelerated recently all over the world. It has become a threat to the stability of the home, the family, and ultimately the church. Mobility results in people living in a community without becoming neighbors, and without getting closely involved. As a result people have fewer personal roots in community life. Since the church often is a community institution, it suffers.

The impact of expressways has also contributed to the tremendous movements of population. From one perspective, the expressway appears to be a "devisive force rather than a new dimension in church planning."[1] Church members who move a distance away can within a few minutes drive back to their home church. This trend has serious implications for the pastor and the church, for it is difficult for the member to assume leadership and to be regular at church functions. The member is faced with the task of traveling the distance several times a week in order to be in church. The distance and the radius of his parish also presents a significant problem to the pastor who desires an efficient and regular program of visitation among the church members. He is forced to decide between evangelistic visitation in the immediate neighborhood of the church and visitation distant from the church where some of the members live.

Anonymity

Impersonal interdependence seems characteristic everywhere. We depend upon others to help us yet we seldom form deep relationships with these many individuals. Time won't permit it. This condition contributes to the depersonalization of individuals in society. People live lonesomely together.

In many places, the adult has been reduced to a "faceless cipher, or a series of [slots] on an IBM card."[2] As a result the adult loses his name and his identity as a dynamic human being in his relationship with men. Hence, the cry that "adults are more than impersonal function, they need to be evaluated [and respected] for who they are as well as what they can do."[3] The depersonalization of people is another reason for the church to be active in reaching people with the gospel. The friendly adult Sunday school class can be the advance guard for evangelism in the church.

Spiraling Knowledge

Increased knowledge is both an asset and a liability. It is an asset because the adult knows more today than in the past. It has helped him to advance in all areas of life. It has helped alleviate the ills of humanity. Aspects of knowledge reach from the minutest reaches of the atom to the farthest reaches of the universe. Man is learning, discovering, classifying, and recording new information at a phenomenal rate. As new discoveries are made, discovery of still newer knowledge is facilitated. So the increase of knowledge poses as a threat to the individual adult because he must keep learning if he is to keep up with the world around him. Keeping current with respect to new knowledge both intellectually and skillfully is difficult.

Increased knowledge also presents problems for the traditional adult Sunday school class. Teachers may be out-of-date in illustrations, language, and understanding of the needs of their students. While not out-of-date in his knowledge of the Word of God, a teacher's application of it can become archaic. If the teacher loses contact with his class, it is difficult to win them to Christ. Most adults want a mental challenge in Sunday school. The teacher must give it and he can, for the Word of God challenges all.

REACHING ADULTS IS IMPORTANT

Increasing Numbers

Throughout the world the number of adults is constantly increasing. Medical advances in science have helped to prolong the life span of adults longer than ever before, and the great youth population soon becomes adult. As a result there is a growing population of adults today.

Strategic Positions

Adults occupy key and strategic functions in homes, business, political, and religious life. For this reason evangelism of adults should be emphasized. More adults should be in Sunday school.

Church Support

Adults are the principal source of leaders for the local church. The financial support for the entire church program comes from adults. Where there is good adult support, the church educational program is bound to succeed and, conversely, where there is little adult support the work limps along and often ultimately fails.

Then, too, adults determine the attendance in other divisions of the church. If adults come they will bring their children, whereas, if children come alone only part of the family is reached. Adults also will take responsibility for leadership and financial support. As a result, they become the backbone of the church, not only in number, but in leadership, experience, and potentialities.

BARRIERS TO EVANGELISM

Formed Habits

Because many adults have crystallized their habits, it is hard for them to establish new habit patterns. However, human nature is essentially modifiable and adults can learn. Every normal human being is a changing creature. This change continues during the lifetime of the person. Adults adjust to new, different, and even difficult situations. Conversion causes a change within the inner being of the person which results in a change of action, words, and way of life.

Hardened Hearts

Adults are not hardened to the call of the gospel. Christ evangelized adults. He won men and women, and their lives were changed. Christ's claim came with force and impact upon mature, intelligent men and women. The Apostle Paul devoted his time in declaring the gospel message to the adult world in Europe and Asia. Adults need God's forgiveness, comfort, and guidance. This is equally true of young and older adults.

Those who are attending when they are establishing their families (25-35 years of age) will probably continue attending through retirement. Therefore, emphasis at the young adult level will pay lasting dividends. Young adults are the least reached group in the church. The young adult has struggled for freedom from his family ties during his teen years and now must form new ties. This struggle in forming new ties represents a lonely and individualistic period of life. Some of the tasks facing the young adult include:

> Forming a mature relationship with a marriage partner.
> Becoming a parent.
> Getting started in a vocation.
> Accepting social responsibility.
> Finding a profound faith.
> These tasks of young adulthood may be summarized as forming mature identifications and assuming mature responsibilities.[4]

This should challenge each church leader to reach young adults. The message comes loud and clear. Reach them, win them, teach them — they are the church of tomorrow.

Older adults often turn to religion and spiritual things. They have time to reflect on the past and the future. Their interest in material things is replaced by a growing concern for spiritual things. The senior citizen can be reached and will respond to the gospel. "The elderly individual is often more open to the message of the church than he has ever been before."[5]

Hesitancy to Attend Sunday School

Many adults have never attended Sunday school and are not familiar with the people, the program, or procedures in the church or Sunday school. Adults fear this new venture because it can cause them embarrassment and a feeling of insecurity. Friendly men and women should greet visitors and help make them a part of the group. Regular attendants must prove themselves friends before they can introduce others to the greatest Friend of all.

Because the educational attainments of some adults are limited, they may have difficulty fully participating in the church's educational program. Some adults have poor reading ability and are embarrassed when they are asked to read in class. The teacher must be sensitive to these feelings. He must seek to know class members and avoid unnecessary embarrassment.

Poor Teaching

The teacher is often the single factor attracting adults to Sunday school. A teacher who knows and likes adults, and has the spiritual gift for teaching is important to evangelism. The church must discover and develop this gifted person and use him. Lessons will be more interesting or stimulating if the teacher uses varied methods of communication. Today's adult is under constant sales pressure. If the adult teacher presents dull lectures, there can be little excitement over Sunday school and little interest in the gospel.

Lack of Interest

Another problem is the wide interest range within the adult class. It is difficult to motivate a class with widely differing interest. Age grading among adults may be the answer. The elective system may be another. Providing a better learning situation will also provide the teacher with fuller opportunity to present clearly the gospel. Life-related teaching is evangelistically productive teaching and is made possible in interest-centered classes.

No Leadership

There must be leadership to promote adult education if adults are to be drawn into the church educational program. Often the impression is given that Christian education is for children because of the priority placed by many church leaders on children and young people in their educational work. Adult leaders must spur the church to improve its adult work and reach this group with the message of evangelism.

SUMMARY

Adults must be reached for Christ and can be through the church educational program. Understanding adults and their unique problems, planning an attractive program for them, and providing good teaching will open many ways to evangelize and make Christ known.

NOTES

1. Lyle E. Schaller, **Planning for Protestantism in Urban America** (Nashville: Abingdon Press, 1965), p. 64.
2. Harvey Cox, **The Secular City** (New York: Macmillan Co., 1966), p. 39.
3. Gibson Winter, **The Suburban Captivity of the Churches** (New York: Macmillan Co., 1962), p. 24.
4. Irene S. Caldwell, **Responsible Adults in the Church School Program.** (Anderson, Ind.: The Warner Press, 1961), pp. 16, 17.
5. Robert M. Gray and David O. Moberg, **The Church and the Older Person** (Grand Rapids: Wm. B. Eerdmans Pub. Co., 1962), p. 37. See also George Lawton, **Aging Successfully** (Columbia University Press, 1946), pp. 167-68. Statistics reveal a higher percentage of older people receive Christ than at the previous age in life.

REVIEW QUESTIONS

1. What three needs of adults influence evangelism?
2. What environmental characteristics cause pressure on adults?
3. Give three major reasons for reaching adults?
4. What are some barriers to reaching adults?
5. Why is adult evangelism often neglected by the church?

FOR DISCUSSION AND APPLICATION

1. Informally ask several adults what they consider their greatest problems to be. Then attempt to determine whether or not belief in Christ would affect these.
2. If you were pastor of a church, what would you consider the responsibility of adult church members was to their unsaved neighbors?
3. Complete the following chart from your church observations.

Adult Concerns	Pressures of Society on Adults	Importance of Adults	Barriers to Reaching Adults

BIBLIOGRAPHY

Dobbins, Gaines S. **Teaching Adults in the Sunday School.** Nashville: Broadman Press, 1936.
Gray, Robert M. and Moberg, David O. **The Church and the Older Person.** Grand Rapids: Wm. B. Eerdmans Publishing Company, 1962.
Jacobsen, Henry. **How to Teach Adults.** Wheaton, Ill.: Scripture Press, 1958.
Towns, Elmer L. **The Single Adult and the Church.** Glendale, Calif.: Regal Press, 1967.

FOUNDATIONS FOR VISITATION EVANGELISM

CHAPTER NINE

Have you ever participated in a church visitation program?
Can you name several people related to your church you should visit this week?
How often do you share your testimony for Christ when you visit others?

Good education communicates the gospel to all who will hear. To do this a program of visitation evangelism should be a part of every church's educational program.

BIBLE EXAMPLES OF VISITATION

Throughout the history of the nation of Israel, God visited individuals. He talked with them, gave them encouragement, and revealed His will. God's visits were personal. He communicated His plans through individuals.

The same emphasis is in the New Testament program of Christ. He set the example of a visitation ministry in homes, in crowded places, and along the wayside. He visited both families and individuals. Since He could not make an evangelistic visit to every community He called and trained disciples to extend His work. He sent His disciples out two by two.

Evangelistic visitation became a program of the apostles. Paul said, "I kept back nothing that was profitable unto you, but have shewed you, and have taught you . . . from house to house" (Acts 20:20). Looking back on the early Church in Jerusalem, we have this statement from the historian Luke, "In every house, they ceased not to teach and preach Jesus Christ" (Acts 5:42).

These records of New Testament visitation imply that the apostles were going to homes with the gospel and that they made an impact on the lives of the people in Jerusalem. Visitation evangelism is one of the most effective methods of giving out the message of salvation to as many individuals as possible.

TYPES OF VISITATION PROGRAMS

Community Canvass

A community canvass enables the church to survey the people of a neighborhood and find potential members. Canvassing is like ground breaking. It helps discover where to apply the real visitation-evangelism ministry of the church. Canvassing is preliminary to a systematic visitation program for the community.

Charles W. Denton suggests the following steps in organizing for a community canvass.

> Select a canvass committee of men and women.
> Map out the areas of the community to be canvassed block by block.
> Set a specific time and date for canvassing.
> Publicize the endeavor in the local newspaper.
> Keep accurate and complete records of findings.
> Immediately follow by evangelistic visitation.[1]

For a community canvass to prove beneficial, an endeavor must be made to reach every home. A friendly courteous greeting will eliminate barriers and encourage the home visited to supply the information needed. Records should be kept of those homes not contacted and an additional visit made. When unchurched homes are discovered, information about children and their ages, or any additional facts revealed, should be recorded for future visitors. Through a canvass church prospects are discovered and the witness of the church extended.

Invitation Visitation

Visitation often is primarily for the purpose of inviting unchurched to church activities. This ministry is carried out by laymen, teachers in church educational activities, and students who call on friends, neighbors, and relatives to invite them to attend church services. Invitation visitation might be connected with a forthcoming VBS, special anniversary service, evangelistic crusade, or the regular activities of the church — especially Christian educational activities which assure continuing contact and opportunity for evangelism.

Evangelistic Visitation

This is for the purpose of bringing the message of salvation to families in their homes. In evangelistic visitation the principles presented in this book to bring people to a point of decision for Christ are applied.

Member Visitation

The three types of visitation already mentioned are planned to contact people outside the church in order to bring them into contact with the gospel. There are other types of visitation, such as absentee visitation, follow-up visitation, and visiting to discuss problems with pupils. Visitation helps the teacher to become acquainted with his students, their homes, and their spiritual needs.

This in turn helps the teacher to orient his teaching to the need of each individual pupil, and thus become a more effective teacher-evangelist.

PREPARATION FOR VISITATION

Organization is essential to the success of a good visitation program. Once a community canvass has been successfully completed, full preparation must be made if visitation evangelism is to be successful. There must be preparation of the church for involvement, preparation of materials for distribution, and preparation of those who will be visiting.

Preparation of Church

A visitation program should be adopted and sponsored by the appropriate board or committee in the local church. It should be supported by the board of Christian education and church action thus giving it church approval and encouragement.

Establishing Church Policy

Sisemore developed the following statement on visitation which may serve as a guideline for pastors and Christian education committees in formulating their own statement on visitation:

> Whereas, we believe that the command of our Lord to go into all the world applies specifically to our local community, and,
> Whereas, we believe that only a comprehensive program of house-to-house visitation can accomplish this purpose,
> Be it hereby resolved,
> 1. That regular, systematic visitation be given a major place in our church life and program.
> 2. That a superintendent of enlargement be elected by the church to plan and direct the visitation of the Sunday school.
> 3. That the absentees be contacted every week by the persons assigned such duties.
> 4. That a master file of all prospects be set up and made available.
> 5. That regular assignments of prospects be made to all officers and teachers and to as many other members as possible.
> 6. That definite reports be made on all visitation.
> 7. That unsaved persons be given full priority in visitation.
> Done by order of the church in regular business session.

_____ Date _____Clerk[2]

Leaders' Example

The support of the pastor and other leaders is essential. If they are excited and sold on the importance of visitation, they will transmit this enthusiasm to the congregation. If they are not concerned for the lost, and do not share in the visitation, the program will have difficulty succeeding.

Enlisting Member Support

Church members must be mobilized to help. Members are first needed to survey the field through canvassing. The people must feel the urgency of evangelism. One concerned layman can motivate many others. Where enthusiasm must be generated, personal invitations to cooperate may be necessary.

Developing Prayer Interest

Organized prayer groups contribute to success. Conversion is the work of the Holy Spirit in and through man. We should encourage members to pray for unsaved relatives and neighbors, and parents to pray for unsaved children. All night prayer meetings have helped some churches. A 12 noon prayer time is another plan which unites members in prayer. Every member of the church, wherever he is, is asked to pause for prayer. Also, members could arrange to pray together at a certain time in a home or a convenient place in school or work. Children and young people should be included in prayer plans. They might especially pray for other youth whom the church is trying to reach.

Establishing the Time

Schedule a definite time for calling. If the day and time for visitation is left to the callers, it might be put off indefinitely. Many Christians want to visit but because of a full schedule or hesitancy do not. Yet they will visit if asked to assist at a given time. There should be a regular day set aside for calling. No other activity should be scheduled in the church. This will make visitation more than just an option. Visitors should be encouraged to reserve visitation day on their personal calendars as well.

Some churches plan a full day of concentrated visitation with the following schedule:

Morning. Workers with cradle roll and preschool children, extension workers, teachers and class officers of adult women's classes meet at church for prayer, instruction, and assignment. They also pick up brochures and other materials to use in visitation. Usually transportation must be arranged and a nursery provided for those with small children so that young mothers may participate. After visitation they may go back to the church for a luncheon.

Afternoon. Another group of those who work with school age children meet at the church and visit boys and girls as they arrive home from school.

Evening. Those who work with young people and adult classes as well as those who are employed away from home can participate in visitation in the evening. They visit from 7 to 9 then return to the church for fellowship, refreshments, and sharing of experiences. This enables visitors to learn from each other and be encouraged by the successes of all.

Total involvement in visitation evangelism is the desire of the local church. Some churches have found that all can be involved by providing a meal at the church. Those who are hesitant to go calling prepare and serve the meal, clean up afterwards, and spend the remaining time in prayer for the visitors. Others serve in the church nursery so husband and wife are able to go calling together.

Preparation of Materials

Provide Literature

The church should prepare informative literature for visitors to use. It should contain an historical sketch of the church — how and when the church began; what the church program is and how it serves people; what its future plans are. Group pictures from Sunday school departments or other agencies such as boys' and girls' clubs, camping program, VBS, and couple activities should be included. People attract people. Pictures should be of groups of people rather than empty buildings. They should show life and activity. One church has prepared an album with 8" x 11" photos showing the church in action. There is a picture for each agency along with an explanation of the service each agency offers. The visitor can take this album along with him to show to the prospects.

The church may also wish to prepare a card or note to leave at the door of homes if people are away.

A home can often be approached by presenting literature showing what the church is doing for the age groups represented. It should include information about the pastor such as education and experience. A picture would also be helpful. This will enable the visitor to have a positive attitude about his pastor. Even when there are some things which might be criticized, a visitor must be sure he does not hinder the person he is trying to reach by criticizing.

Organize a Record System

A card file should be prepared with information regarding each person to be visited. This should include a permanent alphabetized file and a duplicate circulating file. These files will include the following categories:

- Absentees — those to be visited and encouraged to return to Sunday school or other church activity.

- Contacts — those to be visited to make a friendly contact and invitation to attend.
- Prospects — those to be visited to present the claims of Christ.

When a person goes to visit, he should have a clear aim in mind of what he wants to accomplish. Does he simply want to invite the occupant to church, or to make a direct evangelistic appeal. Regardless of his initial aim, however, he always should be ready to witness for Christ.

Absentee Cards. These list the names of those Sunday school students who were absent three times or more. Absentee follow-up may be done by the Sunday school teacher along with one of his pupils. The names of those absent more Sundays should be referred to the Sunday school superintendent and pastor so that they can help solve whatever problem is causing the absence.

There is merit in visiting some pupils the first Sunday they are absent before they get into the habit of missing Sunday school. The visit should be casual, creating in the person a desire to come back. Pray with the pupil before leaving. This may bring a spiritual challenge and refreshment into the heart and home. When the pupil has a good reason for being absent, a telephone call or card is usually sufficient.

Contact Cards. These cards include names of people who have no previous contact with the church. The intent of a visit is to make a contact. The visit is to inform them of the church and its program. Perhaps they are a family contact of a church member. Leighton Ford suggests in his book, *The Christian Persuader,* that each church family be assigned an unsaved family as a personal family project. They are responsible to make friends with the unsaved family, to pray for them regularly, and to invite them to the church services and activities. Usually, church responsibilities rest upon a few men and women, but this can be changed if the pastor would give church families and members "specific targets, persons with whom they could build 'bridges of friendship' across which they could later approach them with a warm Christian witness."[3] Christianity and church membership would mean much more to these individuals.

Prospect Cards. This file lists names of people discovered from the canvass who should be attending; newcomers to the community, visitors at church services, families who have a member attending the church, parents of Sunday school children, youth and children from unchurched homes who come to the church activities and clubs, those who attended VBS, camps, and other meetings of the church. A prospect is someone who should attend church. The first visit after the canvass will determine the accuracy of the preliminary information. It is imperative to visit prospects soon after the census is completed.

Preparation of Visitors
Training

In visitation, as in other skills, it is not just the lessons in the classroom that lead to success but also the time spent with those experienced in the skill. So in the visitation program, a person, to be used by God, needs more than faithfulness in attending classes. One must have experience under proper supervision. The art of successful visitation comes through proper training and patient practice. After the potential visitors are chosen, set aside time for intensive training and study coupled with guided experience. Visitors should know how to approach people, how to guide the conversation, and how to make an appeal. They should also know the doctrinal stand of their church. They should know what they believe and why they believe it.

Personal Qualities

While one must be himself as he endeavors to communicate Christ to others, there is the responsibility to maintain those characteristics which will attract others to the Savior. Appropriate and acceptable dress, which neither attracts to itself nor repels, should be considered.

An alert healthy mental attitude, which is enthusiastic for Christ and reflects the joy He provides, should characterize the believer who would win others.

Spiritual Qualities

While most visitors are not theologians, it is imperative for each to have a Bible-supported personal testimony of faith in Christ. Training should include clear methods of efficiently presenting the plan of salvation and responding to common objections. If possible, the caller should determine possible responses for the most frequent excuses before visiting.

Calling is a spiritual work and will reap everlasting results only when done in the power of the Spirit. The visitor must pray for boldness and insight and for the right words to say. He must be in a prayerful attitude throughout the calling time for we "wrestle not against flesh and blood, but against principalities, against powers, against the rulers of darkness of this world, against spiritual wickedness in high places" (Eph. 6:12).

The visitor who will win souls must also be one who has confidence in the Lord for results. Faith in God's ability to use His people will give new expectations and decisions for Christ. The Lord has promised His personal and abiding presence with those who witness. He will bring results.

SUMMARY

Visitation evangelism is an important ministry in the church educational program. A community canvass should precede visitation. In order to have a successful visitation program, there must be proper preparation of church, material, and visitors. Visitation must be done in the power of the Holy Spirit.

NOTES

1. Charles W. Denton, "Canvassing and Visitation," **Sunday School Encyclopedia**, Vol. IX (Chicago: NSSA, 1959), p. 137.
2. John T. Sisemore, **The Ministry of Visitation** (Nashville: Broadman Press, 1954), pp. 5-17.
3. Leighton Ford, **The Christian Persuader** (New York: Harper & Row, 1966), p. 60. See also Horace F. Dean, **Visitation Evangelism Made Practical** (Grand Rapids: Zondervan, 1957), pp. 77-92.

REVIEW QUESTIONS

1. Name three purposes of a church visitation program.
2. List several steps in organizing a community canvass.
3. How can a church be prepared for a visitation program?
4. Tell the kind of record system a church should have in relationship to visitation.
5. What are the personal and spiritual qualities of a good visitor?

FOR DISCUSSION AND APPLICATION

1. Conduct an opinion poll of church leaders and teachers in which you ask the following questions: Should our church have a visitation program? When is the best time for such a program? In what neighborhood should it be held? How should it be organized? Who should visit?
2. Work with one Sunday school department or church educational agency to help establish a satisfactory visitation program. Include a time schedule, a visitor enlistment plan, and indicate how you would determine who to visit.
3. Describe the content of literature you would want to distribute in a canvass. Secure samples of printed materials and prepare an informative leaflet or sheets regarding your own church program.

BIBLIOGRAPHY

Barnette, J. N. **The Pull of the People.** Nashville: Convention Press, 1956.
Coleman, Robert E. **The Master Plan of Evangelism.** Westwood, N.J.: Fleming H. Revell Co., 1963.
Hyles, Jack. **Let's Build Evangelistic Churches.** Murfreesboro, Tenn.: Sword of the Lord Publishers, 1962.
Kennedy, D. James. **Evangelism Explosion.** Wheaton, Ill.: Tyndale House Publishers, 1970.
Towns, Elmer L. **The Ten Largest Sunday Schools and What Makes Them Grow.** Grand Rapids: Baker Book House, 1969.

THE VISIT CHAPTER TEN

How can a visitation program help your church educational program?
When is the best time for you to make an evangelistic visit?
How do you evaluate the results of a visit?

Churches and their educational activities grow through visitation. They also widen their constituencies and expand their spheres of influence for evangelism. "Visitation is the capstone, the final step in actually reaching people."[1] The ministry of visitation therefore should be given much attention in the educational programming of every church.

ANTICIPATIONS OF VISITATION

The people who visit are often the key to successful evangelism. People are attracted to people. Often the unsaved in a home can be attracted to Christ through a believer's visit. Christian teachers, pupils, and leaders who visit help evangelize those they contact. Many people respond to an invitation to accept Christ after a friendly visit has shown them the meaning of Christianity.

Salvation

Churches long have opened their doors to their communities, but many people do not come of their own accord. Dr. Howard Hendricks states, "The church insults the unsaved with the attitude, come in you lucky sinners and get saved." Many will never receive Christ unless the gospel message is taken to them. Earl Kernahan in his book, *Visitation Evangelism,* asks, "Would it not be better to go to the homes and uncover the religious aspirations and hungers of the individual; question them about local Christian responsibility, and get them to decide to accept Jesus Christ?"[2] Evangelism is the responsibility of every church, every church agency, and every church member. The message of love must be presented with a personal witness and emphasis.

Increase in Attendance

Visitation is the practical application of spiritual concern for men. It not only spreads the gospel but results in sizeable increase in numbers sharing in the church's educational program. Sunday school enrollment increases in proportion to visitation. If a Sunday school is going to succeed, it should have a visitation program.

A growing church will probably have at least one-tenth of its average attendance involved in a weekly calling program. This should be the minimum participation goal of every visitation program. By rotating those involved, a far greater proportion of regular attendants will share in visitation.

While visitation is not a mechanical process which produces results on the basis of mathematical equations, some have indicated that their experience has been that for every fourteen people visited one new person begins attending. This doesn't mean an automatic acceptance at every fourteenth house. However, over an extended period of time a Sunday school might expect to enroll new members at this ratio. Those who go calling can have confidence that God will reward their labors with encouraging results.

THE VISITATION PROGRAM

The possibility of success is increased if the program is begun with a commissioning service on the Sunday immediately prior to beginning a visitation program or the renewal of a visitation project. This gives recognition to the callers, and helps them sense the importance of their assignment. A commissioning service gives an official emphasis to the program because it indicates the whole church is behind it. Also, the Christian attending the commissioning service who is not directly involved in the visitation project may be encouraged to pray definitely for those who are. A commissioning service will increase the interest of the entire church constituency in evangelizing through visitation. The pastor should make the occasion a happy and significant event.

If all meet at the church for assignment, prayer, and supplies before each time of group visitation, the spiritual emphasis so necessary can be shared.

Determining Time

As long as there are callers and there are people in the community, visitation can be successful. In many areas, outdoor activities during the summer make it a difficult time for general visitation. However, vacation Bible school provides challenge and occasion for summer visitation especially if VBS is scheduled for a time when most community children are in the area.

Even bad weather should not thwart a visitation program. Some people may have time to sit down for a friendly talk if visited in inclement weather.

The time of the actual visit must be convenient for the caller as well as the one called on. (Often individual calls can be made throughout the day but a concerted effort must be at a time when most can be reached.) The most convenient hours are usually from seven to nine o'clock on a weekday evening. This provides opportunity for the family to complete the evening meal before the visitor arrives. People tire as the evening progresses and working people as well as the elderly often prepare to retire early.

Communities differ as to convenient times and the purpose of the visit also will affect the time. A canvass may be taken at a different time than an evangelistic visit would be made.

Making Contact

Since visitors will be in teams of two, a strengthening advantage will come from thoughtful discussion of the best approach at each house visited. One of the team should be assigned as the major visitor so that there will not be confusion of emphasis. Before knocking at the door each visitor will want to pray silently for the guidance of the Holy Spirit in what is said and done.

A warm smile and hearty greeting will open many doors. "Good evening, Mr. Jones (call him by name). I am Tom Roberts and this is Sam Parker. We're from Trinity Church and would like to visit with you for a few minutes. May we come in?" Or, "Hello, Mrs. Line. I am Mary Doolittle, and this is Barbara Kale, calling in the interest of your children, Barbara and Tommy (mention names). We've been pleased to have them attend Sunday school and thought it would be good to know their parents." Or, "Hello, Mr. Heller. I am Joe Sanders, and this is Phil Daley. We have a brochure here that explains the work of our church. If you have a few minutes, we would be happy to tell you about it."

It is usually better not to enter the home at the invitation of a child, nor to make a call standing outside the door. Tactfully the visitor should wait to be invited in. If refused, the visitor can present the material he has and proceed to the next house.

If a visitor radiates confidence when making the first approach, acceptance of his message is more possible. A pleasing tone of voice when speaking will also help to make contact. An important message needs to be communicated, so the visitor must be careful to speak slowly and enunciate clearly.

In the Home

Everyone in the home is important. If a sincere interest is shown in each, rapport can be established more easily. It is important to be sensitive to the feelings of the people being visited and share in their joy or sadness.

Often a visitor can find a clue to conversation by appraising the surroundings and observing the general attitude of those visited. This also provides an opportunity to determine ways in which the church might better serve the family. A point of contact might be the home conditions, the children, a hobby, business, or job. By some comment about these interests, the visitor speaks their language and meets the prospect on the level of his interest. The illustrations and language should be able to be understood and sermonizing avoided.

A good visitor must be a good listener. As a man speaks he reveals his interests and also becomes willing to listen. After a hearing has been secured, the gospel can be presented.

The Holy Spirit will guide the conversation if He is permitted to do so. The brochure regarding the church might initiate conversation regarding spiritual matters. An invitation to attend the church services might point out the services or activities that would be interesting to the person. Radiant enthusiasm for the church and pastor will generate interest.

If it is necessary to make arrangements for transportation to the church in order to assure attendance, this should be done. If there is no church bus, the visitor can suggest that he would be glad to drive them to church the following Sunday.

The caller should lay a solid groundwork by a clear explanation of God's Word during the visit. If the caller feels that the person is ready for the presentation of the message of salvation, he should do so.

If the following cautions are observed in witnessing, many discouragements will be avoided.

Share a positive message. Do not argue. No one is argued into belief but many are won when a positive testimony of what Christ has done is presented.

Exalt the Savior. The purpose of the visit should be Christ-centered and exalt Him. The visitor must avoid criticism of other churches, his church, and the people in it.

Practice patience. A successful visitor must be patient and sympathetic. He must maintain poise and keep calm.

Depend on the Holy Spirit. The results are in God's hands. Satan often achieves his greatest work by causing discouragements. Do not be discouraged; the work of God cannot be defeated.

One should not feel he has been unsuccessful if he does not secure a decision during the first visit. A call can be successful without an immediate commitment. Some people may require months of studying the Bible before accepting Christ as their Savior. Others require just a few weeks, and some are converted on the first visit if they have had previous contact with the gospel.

In presenting the way of salvation, present each proposition slowly, step-by-step making sure that the person is following and understands what is being said. The Bible should not be displayed ostentatiously so as to antagonize the prospect but should be used to explain salvation and spiritual truths. Once a person has accepted Christ, he should be encouraged to tell the Lord audibly. This may be followed by the caller's prayer of thanksgiving. Genuine joy with the prospect over his decision will encourage him to continue in his new decision.

Some instruction for Bible reading and prayer might be given plus a pamphlet or literature explaining what it means to be a Christian. Also, some reading material on the privileges and obligations of being a Christian would be helpful. A time should be established to meet and begin the task of follow-up as explained in the following chapter.

Use of Literature

Whether or not the call appears to be beneficial to the person visited or to the work of God, some material with the church name and address and that of the pastor should be given before leaving. If a family is eating, entertaining company, or otherwise busy, this literature may be the only continuing contact. A simple question like "May I mail you some literature on the Bible?" may be the open door to future contacts.

REPORTING AND RECORDING

Report Session

After an evening of visitation, a report session will be a thrilling experience. With the pastor, director of Christian education, or visitation chairman in charge, callers can be given the opportunity to tell of their visitation experiences. Some may have met with problems which were discouraging. Someone else in the group may have experienced the same kind of problem but found a solution about which he speaks and all are inspired and encouraged to try again. Visitors learn from each other what pitfalls to avoid and what techniques to use. The report time might close with a thanksgiving prayer session. Thus encouraged visitors will quickly respond to future visitation times.

Recording Information

Careful records should be kept of all contacts made and these classified according to apparent interest in the gospel. Information shared will assist future callers in knowing how to reach prospects and help the visitation chairman make beneficial assignments. Classifying prospects as "warm," "lukewarm," and "cold" has been suggested by George E. Sweazey.[3]

The warm prospect is a person who is interested in attending church or is willing to discuss spiritual matters. This person should be followed up regularly. The mother and father in one family accepted Christ because the caller returned and presented the same testimony each time. The whole family is attending regularly as a result.

The lukewarm prospect is a person who has attended church but has neglected spiritual matters. He may be indifferent to the presentation of the gospel. This prospect can usually be reached through personal concern. Some churches assign families to the lukewarm prospect and thus reach the whole family.

The cold prospect is a person who has no interest in spiritual matters. He may have had an unfortunate experience with a church member and has rejected Christianity because of it. He can be reached if the person calling on him will be consistent and patient.

The advantage of classifying prospects in categories of this nature helps the caller to be more effective. Materials can be prepared to meet the particular need of the individual. The caller can also be prepared to present intelligently the claims of Christ to those he visits in the light of their background needs.

EVALUATING VISITS

A check list is a good tool to appraise visitation procedures and results. If completed by the visitor himself, the check list can be very beneficial.

Horace F. Dean in his book, *Visitation Evangelism Made Practical,* has proposed the following questions:

1. Was our visit made at the proper time?
2. Did we make the best possible approach?
3. Did the prospect appear to be cordial?
4. How well did I present the purpose of my visit?
5. Did the prospect show definite interest?
6. Is it likely that another visit will be appreciated?
7. Was the way paved for another call and, if so, when?
8. On my next visit, how shall I deal further with the prospect?
9. Am I making my prospect and my work the object of earnest prayer with full dependence upon the Spirit of God?[4]

SUMMARY

Visitation has tremendous potential when properly and carefully planned and carried out by the church. It is a vital way of reaching delinquent church members, church visitors, unchurched relatives and friends, within the local community. Visitation offers a personal touch for contact with lost men and women. Visitation brings results; it insures success in evangelism.

NOTES

1. J. N. Barnette, **The Pull of the People** (Nashville: Convention Press, 1956), p. 105.
2. A. Earl Kernahan, **Visitation Evangelism: Its Methods and Results** (Westwood, N.J.: Fleming H. Revell Co., 1925), p. 21.
3. George E. Sweazey, **Effective Evangelism** (New York: Harper and Bros., 1953), p. 106. See also Autrey, **Basic Evangelism,** p. 84.
4. Horace F. Dean, **Visitation Evangelism Made Practical** (Grand Rapids: Zondervan Publishing House, 1957), p. 54.

REVIEW QUESTIONS

1. Why is it important to go to homes with the gospel?
2. What are the values of a commissioning service prior to a visitation program?
3. List four rules for a visitor to follow to avoid discouragement.
4. What are the benefits of a reporting session after a visitation program?
5. How do records help toward an effective visitation program?

FOR DISCUSSION AND APPLICATION

1. Role play an evangelistic visit to a home with father, mother, and two children busy watching TV when the visitors arrive.
2. Endeavor with others to determine the best time for your church to conduct a visitation program.
3. Imagine yourself as a visitor in a home without Christ. What difficulties might you anticipate? How would you surmount the difficulties?

BIBLIOGRAPHY

Autrey, C. E. **Basic Evangelism.** Grand Rapids: Zondervan Publishing House, 1959.

Edwards, Gene. **Here's How to Win Souls.** Grand Prairie, Tex.: Soulwinning Publications, 1960.

Hyles, Jack. **Let's Go Soul Winning.** Murfreesboro, Tenn.: Sword of the Lord Publishers, 1962.

Little, Paul E. **How to Give Away Your Faith.** Chicago: Inter-Varsity Press, 1966.

FOLLOW-UP OF EVANGELISM

Why should you give extra attention and help to new believers?
Who best can follow up new believers?
How can you help a new convert grow spiritually?

Carefully planned follow-up conserves the fruits of evangelism. The local church leader should help establish the new Christian in the Christian walk. A person may be converted and yet fail in living the Christian life because the one who led him to the Lord did not help him grow spiritually.

Salvation is pictured as a new birth. The converted sinner becomes as a baby in spiritual understanding. He cannot simply be instructed to read his Bible and pray. This short instruction is insufficient. Just as God desires parents to feed, train, and guide the growth of children, so God desires continuing assistance to the one who has experienced spiritual birth.

THE METHOD — BIBLE STUDY

The church Christian education program provides excellent opportunities for follow-up. Here, new converts can search the Scriptures and grow in Christ. God has provided Christians with the Bible. In its message there is strength for those who diligently seek Him. God wants both the new Christian and the more mature to search His Word diligently (Acts 17:11). The Bible is not a systematic textbook or simply a how-to-do-it book. It is written about life and its varied truths apply to the varied lives of those who study it.

The book of I Thessalonians can be considered a follow-up letter written by Paul to Christians, many of whom had been converted less than two months. This letter was written to people much like men today who turn to God and need help to grow spiritually. Paul became their instructor and they looked to him for spiritual food. He shared God's message with them and encouraged them to please God.

THE GOAL — GROWTH

Follow-up conveys the idea of helping someone grow in the Christian experience. This follow-up, therefore, is done after one has accepted Christ as Savior.

Follow-up is bringing a person to spiritual maturity. God expects a Christ-like life which produces fruit of the Spirit (Gal. 5: 22, 23), and victory over sin (I Jn. 2:1). The decision of faith is only the beginning of the Christian life. "For by grace are ye saved through faith" (Eph. 2:8). Faith alone saves, but saving faith is never alone (James 2:22). The Scriptures teach that a Christ-like spirit is a normal thing where people are growing in the Lord. Physically mature people are natural in community life. It should be equally natural to see spiritually mature persons in churches. If new converts are helped to grow to a fruitful, victorious life, there will be more mature Christians in church.

A young businessman professed Christ. The teacher gave him instruction on how to study the Word of God, how to pray, and how to witness. Within six weeks, five people at his office had accepted Christ. It was only normal for the young businessman to witness, but he was guided to successful witness by the teacher's follow-up instructions.

PRINCIPLES OF FOLLOW-UP

Special care must be given to young Christians who need to grow in faith. There are certain principles that can guide a teacher in his relationship to young Christians and make growth more possible.

Since God has given the privilege of leading a person to Christ, we can assume He also has given a responsibility for guiding to growth. The teacher first commits the new child to Christ. But such commitment doesn't relieve him of responsibilities. New parents often commit their babies to God, but still are responsible for their spiritual, mental, social, and moral nurture. So the teacher now becomes responsible for spiritual growth.

Be Personally Involved

Follow-up is primarily personal. Follow-up must be done by someone, not by something such as a class or a church. Too often we leave follow-up to preaching, attending a group Bible study, or other forms of Christian influence. Children are brought up personally — by parents. They are seldom left to provide for themselves in this world.

Paul personally followed up young believers. He visited them on several occasions and encouraged them in the Word of God. The Epistles are filled with prayers for young Christians. Paul followed up young believers through his prayer life. Also, many Epistles are follow-up letters. Paul wrote to these young Christians attempting to meet their needs. He also sent messengers to them when he couldn't go. This was a form of follow-up.

What if God should limit the number of spiritual offspring to those for whom we would take time to care? God seldom gives the natural family more than one child at a time. Capable teachers can care for more than one convert at a time but since follow-up is personal, God may limit the number of offspring to those for whom believers are willing to care.

An aim of Sunday school is to nurture new Christians into spiritual maturity. Sunday school classes should be more than places where Bible facts are communicated or offerings are taken. Paul speaks of the young Christians in Thessalonica, "So being affectionately desirous of you, we were willing to have imparted unto you, not the gospel of God only, but also our own souls, because ye were dear unto us" (I Thess. 2:8). Paul wanted the young Christians to have the same spiritual life that he had. He wanted them to grow. Sharing becomes the predominant theme in follow-up.

Meet Individual Needs

God is concerned with the life of the new Christian. "As ye have therefore received Christ Jesus the Lord, so walk ye in him" (Col. 2:6). Whose fault is it, if the new convert doesn't walk in Christ? It is not the Lord's fault. Nor can the responsibility be shifted to the new convert. If the new believer does not grow in Christ and the teacher did not follow-up, he has to share some of the blame. To properly nurture children, parents must know their habits, diet, and how to care for their basic needs. A new baby needs love and affection. Just as parents have an idea or goal in life for their children, so the teacher-evangelist must know where to direct growth in Christ toward spiritual goals.

Individual needs will be more easily determined through a visit in the home than in the church surroundings. Visitation should be used in follow-up. If time is given to praying together and spiritual counsel of problems, a visit will provide opportunity for guidance in growth not possible in the church.

Be Consistent

The teacher must live what he is attempting to teach. Paul never apologized for asking people to follow his example. "Be ye followers of me, even as I also am of Christ" (I Cor. 11:1). Also he stated, "Those things, which ye have both learned, and received, and heard, and seen in me, do" (Phil. 4:9). The teacher-evangelist also should be able to suggest that the young Christian follow his example. This may be true in ways of spiritual growth as well as daily living.

Paul lists the spiritual gifts of which the last in the list is teacher (Eph. 4:11). The purpose of this gift is revealed in the next verse, "For the perfecting of the saints" (Eph. 4:12). The word *perfecting* means "mending of the net." The work of the church could be pictured as a large net that is thrown into the sea to catch fish. The net with holes will allow many fish to slip through. The Sunday school teacher who is following up more than one pupil broadens his outreach of evangelism. He is mending the net (the class) so that a multitude can be reached for Christ. Hence the teacher who keeps his net mended through follow-up is the effective teacher-evangelist.

FOLLOW-UP EMPHASES

Permanent and constructive evangelism rests upon a thorough program for instruction and growth.

The leader should establish a lasting friendship with the new convert. Rapport must be established between the new convert and the pastor and a personal conference arranged. The pastor is the shepherd of the flock and will want to help the new convert in any way possible. If the pastor has a class for new converts, enlist the young Christian.

The pastor's instruction class usually deals with the church's doctrinal standard. The follow-up on a private basis should deal with practical matters. As someone stated, "We have been so busy telling people *what* to believe, they don't know *how* to believe." Personal follow-up through the church educational program should give them the help they need to live a Christian life.

The primary emphasis of our Lord's ministry was devoted to instruction of his followers. The primary emphasis of the church educational program should be the training of believers, developing them into leaders willing and able to serve. This training takes both instruction and proper guidance. "As ye have therefore received Christ Jesus the Lord, so walk ye in him: Rooted and built up in him, and stablished in the faith, as ye have been taught, abounding therein with thanksgiving" (Col. 2:6, 7). Materials to assist in establishing the new convert are suggested at the end of this chapter.

Assurance of Salvation

Carefully go over the plan of salvation with the young convert. Any matters which have caused questions should be clarified. Emphasize that salvation is not based upon feeling or emotion but faith. Examine with him some Scripture portions such as Ephesians 2:8, 9; Romans 5:1; I John 5:13; and John 6:37 to provide assurance of his salvation.

Dedication of Self

The new convert must be taught that by right of creation and purchase by Christ's blood on Calvary, he belongs to God. Therefore, Christ is entitled to his best in life and service (Rom. 12: 1, 2). This giving of himself will include his time, talents, and finances.

The power of the Holy Spirit is to be appropriated by the new believer. He must be taught how to appropriate this power which will enable him to witness, resist temptation, and to live the Christian life.

The subtlety of temptation must be made clear. Temptation is not necessarily sin, but yielding to temptation is. All believers are tempted, young and old alike. Christ indwells the new believer by the Holy Spirit and will help him to be victorious over temptation (I Cor. 10:13; Acts 1:8).

Study of the Bible

The new convert must be taught the importance of Bible reading and study (Ps. 1:1, 2; Josh. 1:8). Strength will be gained when the Bible is studied and applied to life. During a follow-up visit, the leader and convert should study together, going over problems, and sharing insights they have received from personal study. A person should study for his own personal benefit (devotional study), but also study the Word in detail in order to understand how God has dealt with man through the centuries.

Power of Prayer

The new Christian should be instructed in prayer (Phil. 4:6, 7). When the young believer and leader meet for follow-up instruction they should spend some time in prayer. As the leader opens his heart to God in front of the new convert, an attitude is communicated. Prayer should be acknowledged as conversation with God. The new believer will learn to pray only by praying. He should be encouraged to participate in the prayer service of the local church.

Fellowship With Believers

The new convert should be taught why the church exists and why he should join a local church. He should understand the meaning of baptism and that it is commanded by God (Matt. 28: 18-20). As the new convert becomes a member of the church, he joins a fellowship of believers of like intention and desire. Through membership, the church becomes the spiritual home of every new member. This fellowship will encourage his faith.

Active Witness

The young Christian must be led into an active witnessing ministry. Christ demands man's cooperation in the task of reaching others. "Go ye" (Matt. 22:9), "Go and teach" (Matt. 28:18-20), "Do" (Jn. 4:34), "Witness" (Acts 1:8). These are Christ's commands.

The best way to introduce the new convert to an active witnessing ministry is to go with him on visitation. This will provide the confidence he will need. He also needs to be introduced to the many and varied ways to share faith. Home Bible study, afternoon teas, tract distribution, dinner invitations, showing a film in the backyard are some of these. Showing how these are done is more meaningful than telling about them.

An active witnessing Christian is more than a person who goes out of his way to tell others about Christ. He lives Christ and walks in such an intimate relationship that his victories are shared as easily as the weather is discussed.

SUMMARY

Christian maturity is achieved through an aggressive program of Bible study and personal involvement in the Christian walk. Leaders in a local church must be examples to the new Christian if there is to be a successful follow-up program. Example will be set in assurance of salvation, dedication of self, prayer life, fellowship with the brethren, and active witness. Only when this is so will the new convert grow as he should.

SUGGESTED FOLLOW-UP MATERIAL

Horace F. Dean, **Visitation Evangelism Seminar** (Chicago: Moody Press, 1962).

C. S. Lovett, **Soul-Winning Made Easy** (Baldwin Park, Calif.: Christian Supply, 1958).

Darwin E. Merrill, **This New Life of Yours** (Denver: Baptist Publications, Inc., 1966). Available in three editions, one for children, one for youth, and one for adults.

Waylon B. Moore, **New Testament Follow-Up** (Grand Rapids: Wm. B. Eerdmans Co., 1963).

Marjorie Soderholm, **Salvation . . . Then What?** (Minneapolis: Free Church Publications, 1968).

REVIEW QUESTIONS

1. What methods of follow-up can be used today?
2. In what ways does a follow-up program benefit a church?
3. In what ways did the Apostle Paul follow up new believers?
4. What are the basic principles to be observed in follow-up?
5. What are the primary emphases to be made to the new believer?

FOR DISCUSSION AND APPLICATION

1. If possible, attend a class for new converts in any church. Observe ways in which the believer is helped and ways in which the church organization is advanced. Evaluate the benefits.
2. Compare the help you received as a new convert with the follow-up new believers now receive in the church you attend. What additional helps would be beneficial?
3. Secure copies of follow-up material used by your church and by other groups. Evaluate its possible usefulness to a new believer.

CHAPTER TWELVE

PRAYER
IN EVANGELISM

Why are prayer and evangelism inseparable?
How will praying for the unsaved help your spiritual condition?
How will prayer help you evangelize?

Prayer has been prominent throughout the history of the church. Great men of God have been great men of prayer. They knew travail of soul in the secret place. These men served God well. They were great men in service because they were great men on their knees.

Without prayer the teacher-evangelist is making his task difficult and, at times, impossible. Chafer's book, *True Evangelism*, emphasizes winning souls through prayer. In it he says, "While the work of saving the lost must ever be a divine undertaking accomplished only through [Christ's] finished work on the cross, there are aspects of the work of seeking them which are committed to his followers . . ."[1] This is the Christian leader's privilege and responsibility as he seeks to reach individuals for the Lord, but it must not be done by human effort. Prayer is the bridge between divine sovereignty and man's initiative in winning souls to Christ.

There is no excuse for the spiritual poverty in much Christian educational work today. The power for accomplishing a spiritual work is at the disposal of the Christian. Paul, under the inspiration of the Holy Spirit, wrote, "Praying always with all prayer and supplication in the Spirit, and watching thereunto with all perseverance and supplication for all saints" (Eph. 6:18). The comprehensiveness of prayer is seen in the use of "always" and "all" throughout the verse. Prevailing prayer must be constant and persistent.

IMPORTANCE OF PRAYER

Commanded

A quick survey of the Scriptures will indicate numerous commands for Christians to pray. "Call unto me, and I will answer thee, and show thee great and mighty things, which thou knowest not" (Jer. 33:3). "Pray without ceasing" (I Thess. 5:17). "Be careful for nothing; but in everything by prayer and supplication with thanksgiving let your requests be made known unto God" (Phil. 4:6).

It is evident that prayer has a basic place in the program of God. It enables the believer to unite with God's purposes. Through prayer the teacher is dealing directly with God. Prayer is the channel through which he labors to win his pupils to Christ.

Exemplified

By Old Testament Bible Characters

There are numerous examples of prayer stalwarts in the Bible. Abraham, the friend of God, interceded in behalf of Lot. Joshua prayed for the sun and moon to stand still until God's people put their enemy to flight. Jacob was a man of prayer, who believed in the God of prayer. Moses was called a mighty intercessor. Often his prayer would offset the terrible stroke of God's wrath upon the rebellious nation of Israel. Elijah so stayed the course of nature through prayer that James exhorts Christians to pray as Elijah prayed (James 5:17). Prayer brought health to King Hezekiah. Great and widespread repentance happened among the people of Israel as the result of Ezra's prayer. He was the great mover in a great work for God. Nehemiah is another example of building through prayer. His prayer and the walls of Jerusalem went up side by side. Daniel was first and foremost a man of prayer. His prayer broke the plot of formidable politicians who lobbied against him. He prayed not only in time of crisis but made prayer a daily practice. Men of the Bible prevailed in God's work because they persistently and consistently persevered in prayer. The work of evangelism through Christian education can prevail today if leaders will pray.

By Christ

The Gospels indicate prayer is the foundation of our Lord's method in every undertaking. "The prayers of Jesus discover to us the wellspring of his wisdom and power, the soul of his method, and the root and recipe of all life lived under the smile and by the power of God."[2]

Jesus lived a life of prayer. Jesus is our authority and example in prayer. Prayer was important to Him. Notice how He taught His disciples to pray. He took time to show them how to compose their prayer (Luke 11:2-4). In John, chapters 14 through 16, we are given the formula of prevailing prayer. Christians are exhorted to ask in Jesus' name. This is not a mere magical affix of His name to our prayers, but it is only in the person of Jesus that we have access to the Father. He honors our requests because Christ is our basis of approach to God.

The terms "pray" and "prayer" are used at least twenty-five times in connection with our Lord in the brief record of His life in the four Gospels and His praying is mentioned in other places where the words are not used. The Gospels record seventeen instances of prayers in His life. His earthly life reveals to us this dynamic for Christian service and witness.

The Lord spent time in prayer, "And in the morning, rising up a great while before day, he went out, and departed into a solitary place, and there prayed" (Mk. 1:35). Also, he set aside a place for prayer, "And it came to pass in those days, that he went out into a mountain to pray" (Lk. 6:12).

His brief earthly ministry was saturated with prayer. Even more important is His present risen ministry. "Wherefore he is able also to save them to the uttermost that come unto God by him, seeing he ever liveth to make intercession for them" (Heb. 7: 25). Christ is at the right hand of God praying for believers as they live on earth (Rom. 8:34).

By Paul

Prayer was also the mighty dynamic in Paul's life. Paul S. Rees writes, "If this man Paul was mighty and massive as a man of thought, and as a man of action, and as a man of vision, and as a man of eloquence, he was mighty and massive also as a man of prayer."[3] Paul's various Epistles are filled with prayer. Prayers are written into the paragraphs of his letters (Eph. 1:16 ff.; 3:14-21). He also exhorts Christians to pray.

VALUES OF PRAYER IN EVANGELISM

Prayer is the basis for a life-changing ministry. The history of the Christian church is a history of answer to prayer. The first church in Jerusalem was born through prayer. The first converts in Europe were led to the Lord by Paul and his companions at the place of prayer (Acts 16).

Take prayer out of any Christian work, especially evangelism, and it is the undoing of that work. Victories are won on the knees of God's servants.

Prepares the Teacher-Evangelist

"Pray ye therefore . . ." (Lk. 10:2) is not a request, but a command from the Lord. Remember to pray. Keeping in touch with God is the teacher's main assurance of succeeding in evangelism.

Prayer causes self-inspection. Earnest praying will cost one his easy and self-indulgent habits. Prayer requires confessing and forsaking personal sins. It demands cleansing from the defilement of sin, thus bringing the teacher in right relationship with God.

Prayer encourages confidence. Prayer helps the teacher to be bold in his witness. By prayer the timid teacher is given courage to speak for Christ. The early Christians prayed for boldness (Acts 4:29) and God answered. As a result, the ministry expanded. Prayer will give the teacher a ring of certainty, authority, and conviction in both his teaching and evangelism.

Prayer sharpens understanding. Prayer gives the teacher keen insight into the needs of each of his pupils. Insight is the unusual faculty to "distinguish not only between good and bad, but between good and better, between better and best."[4]

Prayer clarifies methods. Prayer guides the teacher to the right person and enables him to make the right approach, and say the right word when seeking to win a pupil to Christ. Thus the responsibility of persevering in prayer is laid on the teacher in order to get results in prayer. Soul winning cannot be hurried; it takes time. The soul winner must invest time in prayer to get results. It is the man who withdraws in prayer who draws men to God.

Relates to the Holy Spirit

Prayer releases spiritual power. Prayer enables the teacher to exercise his natural gifts as energized by the power of the Holy Spirit. The best curriculum materials or the teaching ability of a teacher is hampered in achieving a spiritual goal without prayerful preparation. If any teacher could influence people by sheer intellectual knowledge and natural gifts, Paul was that man. But Paul urged Christians to pray for him that he might be given utterance, and that he might speak clearly and fully.

Prayer unlocks the meaning of Scripture. Communicating the Word of God as a means to salvation is emphasized in the Scriptures (Rom. 1:16; Heb. 4:12; Rom. 10:14, 15). The human instrument is needed in the proclamation of the gospel. But more than this, the Holy Spirit is the One who wields this mighty sword, who interprets the Scripture. Divine truth has no life-giving ministry apart from the life-giving energy of the Holy Spirit. As the teacher prays and explains the gospel, the Holy Spirit is the agent who unlocks the meaning of Scripture and vitalizes its message. The Word is the sword that must pierce to the dividing asunder of soul and spirit (Heb. 4:12), but it must be the Holy Spirit who interprets it to be effective (Jn. 14:26).

Prayer prepares the unsaved. One of the gripping pictures of the unsaved pupil is the analogy of blindness. Paul paints this picture rather vividly, "But if our gospel be hid, it is hid to them that are lost: In whom the god of this world hath blinded the minds of them which believe not" (II Cor. 4:3, 4).

Chafer writes that this "blinding or unveiling of the mind . . . causes a universal incapacity to comprehend the way of salvation, and is imposed by the arch-enemy of God in his attempts to hinder the purpose of God in redemption."[5] Sometimes the blindness causes men to think the gospel is foolishness (I Cor. 1:18).

God's work of removing blindness includes conviction of sin and illuminating of a man's mind to see his sinful condition, recognize Christ's death on the cross, and seek God's forgiveness. This is the work of the Holy Spirit in answer to prevailing prayer.

EFFECTUAL PRAYER IN EVANGELISM

Prayerlessness can paralyze and short-circuit the church's effectiveness. Advertisement, public relations, and promotional activities are poor substitutes because God's power for soul winning comes through prayer.

The remarkable outpouring of God's Spirit is granted only to the church in which God's people "humble themselves, and pray, and seek [his] face" (II Chron. 7:14).

God's Power

Prayer declares our inability to do the work of God. Therefore, we invoke His power for our ministry of winning souls. God is looking for those who are willing to be partners with Him in bringing the lost into the knowledge of Jesus Christ.

The teacher who bears the name of Christ becomes his representative. He is privileged to use the name of Christ in his intercession. The name signifies the person. We come to God through the person of Jesus and have power with God.

Teacher's Spiritual Condition

By virtue of the Christian teacher's relation to God, he must share the burden of evangelism through prayer. Certain conditions must be met for answered prayer. We are reminded, "God never mocks us by demanding impossible conditions."[6] If we meet his conditions, He will answer our prayer and men will be born again.

Disobedience is rebellion against God. It hinders the Holy Spirit's work through the teacher. Those who abide in Jesus (Jn. 15:7), are promised answers to prayer for prayer and obedience go hand in hand.

H. Clay Trumbull differentiates between faith in prayer and prayer in faith. He said, "Prayer in faith is a commanded duty;

faith in prayer is not commanded, nor is it justifiable. Prayer in faith is always reverent and spiritual. Faith in prayer is too often superstitious and presuming . . ."[7] Therefore, the teacher should not trust in his ability to pray, but trust in God who answers.

Faith is more than intelligent belief and trust. It is an exercise of reaching out to God in faith, confident that He will hear and answer prayer. Often we limit God's answer to our prayers by our unbelief. Faith trusts God and receives from Him.

Our Lord was not pleased with the insincerity of the Scribes and Pharisees. He was able to discern beyond their words when he said, "This people draweth nigh unto me with their mouth, and honoureth me with their lips; but their heart is far from me" (Matt. 15:8). David prayed, "Thou desirest truth in the inward parts" (Ps. 51:6). God puts a premium upon a cleansed heart and life that must approach Him in prayer.

Expectancy is one of the conditions of prayer. An expectant person is an optimistic person. When one is eagerly awaiting God's answers to his petition, the atmosphere is electric and alive with hope. "What things soever ye desire, when ye pray, believe that ye receive them, and ye shall have them" (Mk. 11:24). A teacher must believe that God will save the pupils in his class and go to Him with that expectancy.

PRACTICAL ASPECTS OF PRAYER IN EVANGELISM

A Time for Prayer

The teacher who waits for extra time for prayer will not find it. Life is usually too busy. It takes planning and effort to find time for prayer. Things that one must do are given place in the daily timetable. Remember to schedule prayer time. Prayer is conflict and the average person does not desire conflict. When prayer time has been set aside, the teacher must be regular and systematic in praying. This time must be carefully guarded against intrusions.

Do not hurry an interview with God. It may be fatal to prayer or lead to weak and feeble convictions and inadequate preparation for witness.

A Place for Prayer

The teacher needs a place for private intercession. Actually the location is not important because one can enter into fellowship with the Divine and touch God in faith anywhere and anytime. But for a regular practice of prayer, it is helpful to have a regular place where one can enter and not be disturbed. Here one can concentrate and travail for souls. Here the teacher can pray for victories.

A Prayer List

Without a prayer list, one is apt to ramble in prayer. A prayer list enables one to pray intelligently for a particular pupil and his needs. Often the class roll book can be used as a prayer guide.

Continual Prayer

A prayer that gets answers must be a continuing prayer (I Thess. 5:17). We are not to faint or give up when we are praying for the salvation of our students. Ours is the responsibility. "Ask, and it shall be given you; seek, and ye shall find; knock, and it shall be opened unto you" (Matt. 7:7). The language of the original text tells us to keep on asking.

United Prayer

It is not the amount of prayer, but the attitude back of prayer that brings answers. However, God must be delighted to see people bank together in prayer. "That if two of you shall agree on earth as touching any thing that they shall ask, it shall be done for them of my Father which is in heaven" (Matt. 18:19). Concerted prayer encourages the faith of others.

SUMMARY

Prayer is more than a way of opening a lesson or closing a class. Prayer must have more place in the life of the teacher-evangelist than a short time of intercession in the classroom. The teacher must plead *for* souls before he pleads *with* souls.

As prayer warriors, it would be well to bear in mind what Albert Simpson Reitz expressed in song:

> Power in prayer, Lord, power in prayer
> Here 'mid earth's sin and sorrow and care;
> Men lost and dying, souls in despair;
> O give me power, power in prayer!
>
> Living in Thee, Lord, and Thou in me;
> Constant abiding, this is my plea;
> Grant me Thy power, boundless and free;
> Power with men and power with Thee.

NOTES

1. Lewis S. Chafer, **True Evangelism** (Wheaton Ill.: Van Kampen Press, 1919), p. 3.

2. John Henry Strong, **Jesus the Man of Prayer** (Chicago: The Judson Press, 1945), p. 15.
3. Paul S. Rees, **Prayer and Life's Highest** (Grand Rapids: Wm. B. Eerdman's Pub. Co., 1956), p. 11.
4. Griffith Thomas, **The Prayers of St. Paul** (Edinburgh: T & T Clark, 1914), p. 132.
5. Chafer, **True Evangelism**, p. 57.
6. Louise Harrison McGraw, **Does God Answer Prayer?** (Grand Rapids: Zondervan Pub. House, 1941), p. 165.
7. Henry Clay Trumbull, **Prayer: Its Nature and Scope** (Philadelphia: John D. Wattles & Co., 1896), p. 53.

REVIEW QUESTIONS

1. Give scriptural examples of the importance of prayer.
2. In what four ways does prayer prepare the teacher-evangelist?
3. How does prayer relate to the work of the Holy Spirit?
4. How does a teacher's spiritual condition affect prayer?
5. List five practical aspects of prayer in evangelism.

FOR DISCUSSION AND APPLICATION

1. Inquire from several believers what part prayer had in their salvation. In cooperation with others in the class, compare the answers of those interviewed.
2. Gather a group of believers in prayer for specific individuals. Invite each to pray for a person to whom he has been witnessing or desires to witness.
3. Keep a prayer list, a prayer schedule, and a prayer record for one week. At the end of the week, evaluate your prayer activities.

BIBLIOGRAPHY

Chafer, Lewis Sperry. **True Evangelism.** Wheaton, Ill.: Van Kampen Press, 1919.